W9-BCF-317

ELIJAH

AND THE RAVENS OF CARITH

A Twenty-First Century Reflection
in a Medieval Carmelite Mode

Michael Dodd

Elijah and the Ravens of Carith

© Michael Dodd, 2009. All rights reserved.

Pileated Press
E9715 Berry Road
Wisconsin Dells, WI 53965-9609
pileatedpress@wisconsin.usa.com

Cover Design by Thomas Scharbach

ISBN: 1442169249
EAN-13: 9781442169241

No part of this book may be reproduced or transmitted in any form or by any means, graphic, electronic, or mechanical, including photocopying, recording, taping, or by any information storage retrieval system, without the written permission of the author.

Dedicated with love and gratitude to
Fr. Sam Anthony Morello, O.C.D
and to my own special ravens:
Dino, Jim, Rick, Steve,
Michelangelo and
Tom

Zelo zelatus sum
pro Domino Deo exercituum

With zeal have I been zealous
for the Lord God of hosts.

I Kings 19:10

Motto of the Carmelite Order

Contents

Michael Dodd was a Discalced Carmelite for over thirty years and has written and lectured extensively about Carmelite history and spirituality. He is an instructor in the Distance Learning Program in Carmelite Studies of the Carmelite Institute in Washington, D.C.

His other books include *Jerome Gratian: Treatise on Melancholy* and a novel, *The Dark Night Murders: A Fray John of the Cross Mystery*.

Preface

The prophet Elijah is one of the most fascinating figures among the whole multitude of characters in the Bible. His story appears in the Books of Kings in the Old Testament, where he works wonders before disappearing into heaven in a chariot of fire. There is even an excerpt from a letter attributed to him in 2 Chronicles 21:12-15, although since it dates from after the time of his ascension, it seems unlikely that the attribution is reliable.

Elijah is, however, clearly lauded in the Book of Ecclesiasticus (Sirach), and his return is prophesied in the last verses of the Christian version of the Old Testament, in Malachi 4:5-6:

> *See, I will send you the prophet Elijah before that great and dreadful day of the LORD comes. He will turn the hearts of the parents to their children, and the hearts of the children to their parents, lest I will come and strike the land with a curse.*

That promised return haunts the accounts of John the Baptist in the gospels, and some would say that Elijah lurks in the background of the portrayal of Jesus in the Gospel of Luke and the Acts of the Apostles, presumably penned by the same author. Elijah represents the entire prophetic tradition when he appears beside Moses at the Transfiguration of Jesus on the mountain in all three of the synoptic gospels. Paul mentions him in the letter to the

Romans (11:2) as does the letter of James (5:17).
Elijah is also generally assumed to be one of the
mysterious dying and rising witnesses in chapter 11
of the Book of Revelation. No Old Testament
prophet, in fact, is referred to in the New as often as
Elijah.

He is a recurring figure in the stories of
rabbinic Judaism, medieval Christianity and Muslim
spirituality. His feast is commemorated liturgically
on July 20 by Orthodox, Catholic and some
Protestant churches. He has been a popular subject
in art and music, including folk songs, spirituals and
an oratorio by Felix Mendelssohn.[*]

Is it any wonder, then, that throughout the
millennia men and women who sought the Spirit of
God should have found in the stories of Elijah an
exemplar for their quest?

In some of the earliest writings of Christian
ascetics and hermits, one finds references to Elijah
as the model of the consecrated life. An Orthodox
prayer for the feast of St. Anthony of the Desert
(+356) begins, "O Father Anthony, you imitated the
zealous Elijah." The influential *Life of St. Anthony*
written by St. Athanasius contains several allusions
to the Elijah stories, as do the stories of other saints.
A raven was said to have brought a half loaf of bread
daily to St. Paul the Hermit. When St. Anthony
came to visit St. Paul, however the raven brought a
full loaf, and the two argued until nightfall over who

---

[*] For more on the presence of Elijah in these traditions as
well as in the Carmelite spiritual world, see Jane
Ackerman's extensive study, *Elijah, Prophet of Carmel*
(Washington, DC: ICS Publications, 2004).

should bless it. (Apparently each was too humble to want to assume precedence.)

Ravens also appear in stories about other holy men and women. For example, a raven was sent by God to St. Benedict, but not to bring him bread. It came to take a poisoned piece of bread out of his hand. The saint is often depicted with a raven nearby.

St. Meinrad's association with ravens turned the tables on the Elijah model, as it were, for that saint was said to feed ravens daily from his own hands. When he was robbed and murdered, the ravens followed the thieves and by their loud cawing, alerted the neighborhood of the crime. The monastic coat of arms of Meinrad's Einsiedeln Abbey incorporated ravens in its design. These stylized ravens came to America when they were adopted by the Benedictine Abbey of New Subiaco in Arkansas, which has historical roots in the Einsiedeln community as well as the Abbey of St. Meinrad in Indiana.

The prophet Elijah's role as an exemplar of the consecrated life was well established by the time of the Crusades and the arrival of significant numbers of western European Christians in the Holy Land as warriors, clerics, pilgrims and religious. In the early thirteenth century, a group of hermits who had assembled on Mount Carmel, with its powerful associations with the prophet, consciously took him as their spiritual leader, and in a short period had used the scriptural stories of Elijah to elaborate a rich reflection on their own vocation. For some centuries, many of the men and women who followed in the spiritual tradition of these hermits –

called the Brothers and Sisters of Our Lady of
Mount Carmel in the documents of the church –
believed that these stories reflected historical facts.
Perhaps some still believe this in the secret caverns
of their hearts.

Regardless of the history, however, the
treasure of stories has inspired thousands of God-
seekers, including canonized saints and Doctors of
the Church, within the Order of Carmel and within
the larger community of believers. I am convinced
that the stories can continue to speak to us today
when we attend to them with a pondering heart.

In the following chapters, we will approach
one of these stories about Elijah with the spirit of the
early hermits on the holy mountain, in a manner
reminiscent of the way Christian contemplatives for
many centuries have come to scripture in the
exercise of *lectio divina*, divine reading. We will
first look at the story itself, specifically the call of
Elijah to hide himself in the Wadi Carith to drink
from the stream and be fed by ravens. Then we will
ponder elements suggested by the story: the
experience of spiritual dryness; the meaning of
detachment; charity; the Holy Spirit; the often
unexpected instruments of God's communication;
and transformation through meditation and
contemplation.

For more than three decades, I have been
nourished by the Carmelite tradition and its
reflection on and of the story of Elijah and others
who have sought the One who sent ravens to feed
the prophet in the Wadi and who spoke in that fine
silence outside the cave on Mount Horeb. To the
men and women who have been living echoes of that

10

Voice to me, I express my thanks. Some of you know who you are; others may be unaware of the role that you played in my journey. All of you have been gift.

Chapter One

Elijah at Carith

Elijah the Tishbite, from Tishbe in Gilead, said to Ahab, "As the LORD, the God of Israel, lives, whom I serve, there will be neither dew nor rain in the next few years except at my word."

Then the word of the LORD came to Elijah: "Leave here, turn eastward and hide in the ravine of Carith*, east of the Jordan. You will drink from the brook, and I have ordered the ravens to feed you there."

So he did what the LORD had told him. He went to the Wadi Carith, east of the Jordan, and stayed there. The ravens brought him bread and meat in the morning and bread and meat in the evening, and he drank from the brook.

See *I Kings 17:1-5*

---

* As is noted later, the spelling of the name of the ravine is perhaps as disputed as its exact location: Kerith, Cherith, Carith. I use *Carith* to fit the interpretation given to the name in *The Institution of the First Monks*, found below.

This biblical story introduces the character Elijah into the history of the notorious King Ahab who ruled Israel in the ninth century B.C.E. Ahab is described in the First Book of Kings as "*worse than all his predecessors. The least that he did was to follow the sinful example of Jeroboam son of Nebat: he married Jezebel, the daughter of Ethbaal king of the Sidonians, and then proceeded to serve Baal and worship him.*" (I Kings 16:31)

Despite the Biblical author's condemnation, this alliance with his pagan neighbors seems to have brought prosperity to Ahab, who built an ivory palace for himself and established towns in the countryside. Yet material prosperity was not always a sign of God's favor, as the prophets continually reminded kings, priests and people and as men and women, ancient and modern, continually forget.

> Then the prophet Elijah arose like a
> fire, his word flaring like a torch. It was he
> who brought famine on them, and who
> decimated them in his zeal. By the word
> of the Lord, he shut up the heavens...

> See *Ecclesiasticus [Sirach] 48:1-3*

There is far more to the Elijah story, of course: miracles of an endless supply of oil and flour, the raising of the dead, calling down fire on Mount Carmel, further confrontations with Ahab and the dramatic ascent into heaven in a chariot of fire. All of these stories have provided fruit for reflection, conversion, commitment and worship throughout the

14

centuries for Jews, Christians and Muslims. Our goal, however, is simple, to join the ancient Carmelites in looking at the opening episode of the Elijah stories: the command to go to Carith and there to drink of the spring and to be fed by ravens.

The Carmelite tradition of reflecting on the Elijah story has been preserved for us in a work attributed to John XLIV, Patriarch of Jerusalem in the early fifth century, but apparently actually written in the form we now have by the Catalonian friar, Philip Ribot, toward the end of the fourteenth century. It may well contain older traditions, but so far no written text has been found to antedate the *Book of the Institution of the First Monks.**

What matters to us is that by the time of Ribot, Carmelites used the Elijah story to help themselves understand and express to others their unique calling and place within the church. Their exposition of the Carith experience may have little

---

*

For a book of such spiritual significance for the Carmelite community, and through that community for the church as a whole, it can be a challenge to find a readily available English translation. One always seems to be forthcoming, but never quite arriving. It can be found, however, in *The Ten Books on the Way of Life and Great Deed of the Carmelites (including the Book of the First Monks): A Medieval History of the Carmelites Written C. 1385 by Felip Ribot, O.Carm.*, edited and translated by Richard Copsey (Faversham: St. Albert's Press, 2005).

to do with the actual events of the ninth century before the coming of Christ. It has everything to do with the Carmelite's own self-understanding, as we shall see.

Imagine a thirteenth century Carmelite brother gathering new members of his community around an evening fire to tell them this story. It is about Elijah, but it is the brother's own story, the story of the other experienced brothers sitting around, and perhaps the story of the newest arrival as well. As each one hears the tale, he finds himself in it – not in its details, but in its depth of meaning.

"Ages ago," the venerable brother begins, "centuries before the Blessed Virgin gave birth to the Promised One, the prophet Elijah stood up to confront King Ahab, who was leading the Chosen People of God astray into the worship of the false god Baal, beloved of his evil queen, Jezebel, whose very name has become a curse. Filled with holy zeal, the prophet declared that God was sending a drought upon the land as a sign that it was he, the LORD, the God of Israel, who was Lord of life-giving rain, not the false Baal who Jezebel and her lying priests claimed wielded the thunder and sent the storm."

The brother pauses to look up at the cloudless sky arching overhead, where stars are beginning to appear against the deep blue of night.

"And God did as the prophet had decreed. The rains ceased, the rivers dried to streams, streams became empty ravines, ponds became dust-filled hollows and the crops withered in the fields. People began to weep and to moan, and a terrible hunger fell on the whole land of Israel.

"In the midst of this suffering, God cared for his prophet. The word of God came to Elijah and instructed him: '*Leave this place, turn eastward and go hide yourself in the Wadi Carith, beyond Jordan. There you will drink from the brook, and I have ordered the ravens to feed you.*'

"And Elijah did as he was told and went to Carith and hid there, and the ravens brought him bread and meat in the morning and bread and meat again in the evening. And he drank from the brook that flowed in that place."

The brother pauses for a moment and leans back. Bright eyes fix on him in the darkness, the eyes of the youngest brothers. The elders have closed their eyes, lulled into calm by the familiar words. The youngest, however, lean forward lest they miss a word. They have heard the story before, but then it had seemed just another tale the priest told. Now they sense that it is more than a piece of the past. The story is taking on a new life in their hearing it around this fire as this night falls.

"Now, my brothers, that, if you will, is what happened. But what does it mean? Why did the sacred writer bother to record this story?"

The speaker looks around, pausing a second to gaze into the eyes of each one in the circle before he continues.

"Because it is meant for us, for you, today. And here is what it means for those of us who are called to live the life of allegiance to Jesus in the way of Elijah.

"First," he holds up his hand with fingers outstretched and points to his thumb, "we are told to leave here – that is, to depart from the temptations and evils of the world around us. This is our first step. But we must not just leave that behind," and he points to his index finger "– we must go somewhere else – eastward, towards the rising sun, the source of light." His middle finger: "And we must hide ourselves in Carith – that is, in charity, love. There we will find the life-giving spring which is the Holy Spirit, welling up within us, as the Lord himself says in the Gospel of John." The next finger: "We will drink of that spring of life and enlightenment." Finally he touches his little finger. "And we will be nourished by our daily bread in the Eucharist, and in the pondering of the Word, and in the substantial truth of God's will for us, the doing of which is the meat that same Lord spoke of to his apostles when at the well in Samaria. The ravens are the ones who bring us this bread and meat – the clergy, our teachers, our companions, other people, and the events of our lives."

He leans back, puts his hands on his knees and smiles at the attentive faces and the eyes reflecting the firelight's dance.

"Our part is to ponder these things, and by God's gracious free gift, we are thus given to eat and drink of life everlasting.

"So it was in the days of the prophet; so it is today. Leave all that dry and arid land behind you; hide yourself in the practice of charity; and God will send you bread and meat and drink for the journey."

And with a sigh, he closes his eyes, nodding softly.

"And so it is today," he repeats under his breath.

This way of understanding a passage from scripture was familiar to the Carmelites of the Middle Ages, because it was the method commonly used to interpret the word of God. Whereas modern readers tend to look only for the literal meaning of the scriptures, or perhaps for what (they think) the inspired writer intended to say, the medieval mind looked for more. These hermits gathered on the mountain near the spring of Elijah did not think of stories in the Bible as a kind of divinely sanctioned history. What would be the point of that? The stories must be there to teach a lesson. They would not read or, more likely, hear a story and ask, "Did that really happen?" That was not a live question for them, mainly because they assumed that it had. Instead, they would ask, "What does that mean for me?"

This is often referred to as looking for the *sensus plenior*, the *fuller sense*, or sometimes the spiritual or mystical sense of the scripture. To most people today, that may sound like a license to play fast and loose with the word of God, as if one could twist it to make it mean whatever one wanted. The medieval readers or hearers of the Word, however, saw it quite differently. For them, to reduce the meaning of the scriptures to only the surface account would be somehow to demean the reality of divine inspiration. Respect for the divine origin of the Bible meant one was obliged to seek the deeper meaning, without discounting the literal significance.

As the Carmelite Doctor of the Church, John of the Cross, wrote to Madre Ana de Jesús in the prologue to his *Spiritual Canticle*,

> The wisdom and love of God is so immense, as is said in the Book of Wisdom, that it reaches from one end of creation to the other [8:1] ... It would, therefore, be ignorant to think that expressions of love found in mystical understanding, like these songs, can be well explained in any human words; for the Spirit of the Lord, who dwells within us and aids our weakness, as St. Paul says [Rom. 8:26], pleads for us with unspeakable groans in order to express what we can neither understand nor comprehend completely.*

Although the saint here refers to the commentary he is providing to the stanzas of a poem he himself has written, he is pointing out to the reader that even he, the very author, cannot express or explain fully the meaning of the words insofar as they flow from the Holy Spirit of God. This reminds him of the experience of reading

---

* Unless otherwise indicated, translations of passages from Carmelite authors are my own. All quotations from John of the Cross in this chapter are from the prologue to his prose work usually called *The Spiritual Canticle*.

...those images in the divine Song
of Solomon and other books of Sacred
Scripture where the Holy Spirit, unable to
convey the fullness of the meaning in
ordinary and usual terms, speaks mysteries
in strange figures and likenesses. From
this it follows that even the saintly
doctors, however much they say or might
say, can never finish expounding these
figures and comparisons, as if this could
be told in words. Indeed, usually what
they say in explanation of these
expressions is a small part of what they
contain.

The fact that the Spirit's meaning was
always greater than the human ability to grasp it was
no deterrent to John or others. They saw no reason to
be discouraged. This did not mean one could not
understand at all, but rather that one could always
come to understand more and that more would
remain to be understood. It is not that there is no
revelation; it is that more will be revealed. Not,
notice, something contrary. Something more.

That is why it did not mean that one could
simply twist the meaning to whatever one wished,
although the danger of misunderstanding always
existed. That fear of misunderstanding is what
renders this medieval approach somewhat unsettling
to the modern reader, accustomed to looking only at
the literal meaning, and usually assuming that there
can be only one such meaning. For the ancient
Carmelites and the believers of their day, reading

was not done in the isolation of one's own mind. The guidance of the church in general and one's own spiritual director or other companions helped direct the one delving into the channel of the larger truth to which they must always conform. And that truth was indeed always *larger*.

There was a famous verse that demonstrated the rich meanings to be found in a single story in the sacred writings:

> *Littera gesta docet,*
> *Quid credas allegoria,*
> *Moralis quid agas,*
> *Quo tendas anagogia.*

> The literal sense tells what happened,
> The allegorical what you should believe,
> The moral what you should do,
> The anagogical where you are going.*

The *sensus plenior*, if you will, as illustrated in the imaginary brother's retelling of the Elijah story above, includes all of these. The literal sense is the story of Elijah at Carith; the allegorical sense says that Elijah represents the believer, the wadi represents love and so on; the moral sense tells the believer to imitate the prophet by leaving the world behind and so on; and the anagogical shows that the believer is going toward communion with God in

---

* For further reflection on this approach to scripture, see Thomas Aquinas, *Summa Theologica* I, 1,10

contemplative prayer and love just as Elijah drank of the spring and was fed by the ravens.

In the following chapters, we will look at the story of Elijah at Carith in the spirit of the early Carmelites. Although the Carmelite understanding of the story influences my reflections in ways conscious and unconscious, what I intend to offer are further reflections that begin with some of those elements but may develop them further or even take off in an entirely different direction.

One does not, therefore, need to know any of the details of the Elijah story as it was told in the Carmelite tradition, although a perusal of some of the sources you will find mentioned in the notes and available through the Resources at the end of this volume will undoubtedly enrich your own ruminations on this treasure.

Ultimately my goal is not to provide you with a complete and definitive exposition of either the scriptural account or the medieval midrash.[1] In particular, this is not an attempt to reproduce or to

---

[1] *Midrash*, Hebrew for "study", technically refers to a rabbinic commentary on a text from the Hebrew scripture, based on a homiletic or comparative method of interpretation. Used more broadly, as it is here, it refers to the expansion and interpretation of biblical passages in an imaginative and exhortatory manner. Usually this entails teaching a truth by way of a story.

I am reminded that when I was studying homiletics, we were told, "No concept without a percept." That is, the hearer understands abstract ideas more fully when the idea is linked to a concrete image or story.

Think of the power of the parables of Jesus. Could the truth revealed in the story of the Prodigal Son be stated so effectively in a moral treatise? Or the culturally unsettling message of the Good Samaritan?

comment upon the detailed Carmelite reflection on the Elijah story found in *The Institution of the First Monks.* As the subtitle of this little volume indicates, this is a twenty-first century reflection in the mode of the medieval Carmelite. I will, if you permit the analogy, be playing a modern song on an older instrument, hoping that the combination will yield a richer tone than would either alone.[2]

To return to John of the Cross and his words to Mother Ana de Jesús in the Prologue of his commentary on the verses of the *Cantico espiritual,*

> ... I cannot explain them
> completely, not is it my intention to do so,
> but only to shed a general light on them ...
> I believe this is the better way, to explain
> the utterances of love in their broadest
> sense so that each one may profit from
> them according to one's own manner and
> spiritual capacity, rather than narrow them
> down to a sense that would not
> accommodate itself to every palate. Thus,
> though I give some explanation of these
> stanzas, there is no reason to be tied or
> attached solely to that explanation. For the

A *midrash* is a bearer of truth, but the truth is not so much in the literal details but in the spiritual meaning conveyed through those details.

[2] See Louis Bouyer, *The Meaning of Sacred Scripture* (South Bend, IN: Notre Dame Press, 1958) for a readable presentation of a critical approach to the word of God that respects the literal meaning as understood by scholars today with a search for the underlying Word.

subject of these songs is the mystical
wisdom which comes through love, and it
is not necessary that it be understood for it
to have its loving affect in the soul, for it
comes through faith, in which we love
God despite our lack of understanding.

Just as John was sure that Mother Ana
would be guided by the Spirit of wisdom whom God
granted to her as she read John's words, so I am sure
that the same Spirit of wisdom, residing in the
depths of the reader of these far less mystical words,
will guide each one who is willing to go further into
the Wadi Carith, there to drink of the spring and to
be fed by those God lovingly and surprisingly sends.

Chapter Two

Neither Dew nor Rain:
The Experience of Dryness

"In a real dark night of the soul it is always three o'clock in the morning, day after day."

F. Scott Fitzgerald, *The Crack-Up (1936)*

I suspect that you too have had the *three o'clock in the morning* experience:

I wake up abruptly into dark silence. Even if there is traffic noise outside or the hum of a refrigerator in the kitchen, these just underline the fact that I am alone. My spouse may be gently snoring beside me, the night light in the hall may remind me of children asleep in the room next door. But I, in the most fundamental depth of my being, am ALONE.

But perhaps not alone for long. My mind begins to fill with disturbing thoughts – what some have called "Anxieteers" – about my health, my finances, the future, the war or the election or the latest salmonella scare or what the administrative assistant thinks of me or my boss or why none of it seems to matter and why I have no control over anything and this is not at all what I expected to be doing at this time in my life and on and on and on.

When I was a child, the monsters hid under the bed or in my closet, but now they inhabit my own mind and all the adults are asleep with no one to come and turn the light on to scare them away.

When the three o'clock time comes, I feel thirsty. I creep out of bed and get a glass of water. Or milk. Or something stronger. Anything to get rid of the dryness in my throat, in hopes of getting rid of the dryness in my heart and my spirit. Anything to get back to the oblivion of sleep. The problems don't disappear, but maybe I can escape them for another few hours. After all, as that plucky survivor Scarlett O'Hara famously reminded us, "Tomorrow is another day."

But, as F. Scott Fitzgerald said, it may be three o'clock in the morning, day after day.

This experience of dryness and emptiness comes and goes in life. It is part of the rhythm reflected in nature, where spring is followed by summer and then fall and then a cold, dormant, seemingly lifeless winter. Yet that winter is followed by another spring and on it goes.

"Just hang in there," we tell one another in the dry times, hoping that this one won't be a day-after-day experience. In the words of an old song, there has to be a morning after.

Right?

The Elijah story begins with God sending a drought upon the land to punish the people for their infidelity. So that the prophet himself may escape the worst effects of the drought, God sends him to the Wadi Carith, where a spring continues to flow and where food will be provided by the means of ravens.

A *wadi* is a ravine or valley, often a dry riverbed that contains flowing water only during rainy seasons. It corresponds to what is called an *arroyo* in the American southwest. It is interesting that God would have sent the prophet to such a place, since the brook in such a wadi would inevitably dry up during a period of drought, as indeed the brook at Carith eventually does in the story.

The name of this particular wadi appears in several variations, uniform spelling being a concern of the modern mind and not of the ancients. So we find Carith, Cherith and Kerith. In fact, it is not clear today exactly which ravine is supposed to correspond to Elijah's refuge. Some have associated it with *Wady el-Kelt* near Jericho, where a number of mountain streams come together. Others place the site elsewhere, depending on how one understands the Biblical description of it as *contra Iordanem* – variously translated as "over against the Jordan" or "before Jordan" or "opening onto the Jordan" or even decisively as "east of Jordan."

The subject for reflection, however, in this chapter is not the wadi but the dryness.

In the Elijah story, dryness manifests itself as drought. Drought is an extended period of time – in the Elijah story, it is described as either three years (I Kings 18:1) or three and a half (James 5:17) – during which a geographical area suffers from a deficiency in its usual water supply. Although this may be caused by other factors, the most common is lack of precipitation. This is certainly the case in the story of Elijah, who promises that neither rain nor dew will fall until God responds to the prophet's words calling them forth.

From this perspective, drought appears to be rooted in causes beyond human control, as to some degree it is. Human activity may generally not bring on a drought, but with increasing technology, human activities can cause a risky situation to deteriorate into a disastrous one. Such activities include over-farming, excessive irrigation, deforestation and erosion, all of which have an impact on the ability of soil to retain moisture.

That this need not demand high tech exploitation of resources is suggested by theories of the destruction of the ecology of Easter Island by deforestation as part of the culturally suicidal obsession with erecting the giant stone figures that make the island famous.

With greater technological ability at hand today, even positive efforts to divert the flow of rivers and the construction of vast reservoirs, often intended to help prevent drought in one area, may lead to devastating results elsewhere.

So it is with the dryness that we experience in our spiritual lives. Much of it seems beyond our immediate personal control. The stock market drops, a housing bubble bursts, companies downsize and we find ourselves out of work and with a pension far less generous than we had expected.

A routine visit to the doctor results in questions, some unfamiliar and expensive tests, uncomfortable procedures with discomforting reports. Cancer, a familiar problem in my family, makes another appearance. I had done what the doctors suggested: exercised, did not smoke or drink, watched my diet scrupulously. Yet the scans reveal that all my efforts to avoid this disease have failed.

A beloved son sets off with his lovely young date for a school dance. A father, having just celebrated a business victory over a few beers with friends at a bar, rushing home to surprise his wife and children with the good news, skids on wet pavement and into the car carrying the teenagers. No one survives.

The disruption caused by events such as these is enormous. It will not go away quickly. As the help-wanted ads in the paper become fewer and fewer, as the doctor visits become more frequent and less hopeful, as yet another day dawns without the sound of a voice and the sight of a face, the realization that life is unfair seeps into the fiber of our being.

It comes with many feelings: anger, sadness, denial, fear. And sometimes it comes with guilt.

Perhaps because we are so accustomed to biblical stories such as the Elijah account of the drought, from childhood we come to connect painful experiences with punishment. Of course, there are other causes for this way of viewing suffering. Since most of us have in fact been punished for misbehavior, it is reasonable for us to find a causal relationship between the wrong we have done and the suffering that results. This make take the form of actual physical punishment or the emotional pain of disapproval and its accompanying fear of loss of love. As children, we may not understand that loving parents may feel compelled to punish us but that their love for us is not at risk. Some of us may never feel secure about love or come to trust another fully. This can color our experience of dryness.

One reason to mention this point is that we may be inclined to attribute erroneously all suffering to divine punishment. Sometimes we unconsciously see everything that happens as divine retribution for a specific failing on our part. When people in pain cry out, "Why did this happen?", they usually mean, "Why did this happen *to me*?" And behind this cry lurks another question: "What did I do to deserve this?"

There is even a logical error that may be at work when we think this way: *post hoc, propter hoc*. Fancy Latin for "This happened *after* that, so this must have happened *because* of that." At its most egregious, this is at the root of many superstitions. A black cat crossed my path on the way to school, and that is why I failed the test. I broke a mirror, and that is why I have had a long run of bad luck. Or perhaps because I wore my lucky sox today, I got that contract!

We know better than to believe these things, but studies indicate that Americans in the twenty-first century are susceptible to superstitions. Don't you secretly *hope* those favorable fortune cookies are telling the truth?

This, as I say, is a logical fallacy. The fact that Event A follows upon Event B does not necessarily mean there is a causal (or any other) connection between the two. Yet we frequently assume, speak and even act as though there always were.

While some passages in scripture do indicate a connection between our suffering and our sinfulness, others direct our thoughts in a different direction. The most outstanding example of this is the story of the healing of the man born blind, which can be found in the ninth chapter of the Gospel of John.

> As [Jesus] walked along, he saw a man
> who had been blind from birth. His disciples
> asked him, "Rabbi, was it his sin or that of
> his parents that caused him to be born
> blind?"
>   "Neither," answered Jesus:
> "It was no sin, either of this man
> "or of his parents.
> "Rather, it was to let God's work show
>   forth in him."
>
> John 9:1-3 (New American Bible)

In this story, which is one of the "signs" that distinguish the Fourth Gospel's portrayal of Jesus, he shows the disciples that there can be more than one way of perceiving the same reality. The disciples thought of the man's blindness as a *result* of God's action, based on some human action in the past; Jesus saw it as an *opportunity* for God's action to heal in the present. In the view of Jesus, the power of God is indeed manifest in this situation, not, however, by punishment but by merciful love.

Years ago in Dallas, a social worker friend told me that she had learned that people who find themselves in particularly difficult situations – what I here call dryness, for example – have three fundamental options:

One, they can change the situation.

Two, they can get out of the situation.

Three, they can change their perception of the situation.

The story of the healing of the man born blind is an example of this third option, changing our perception of the situation.

Too often we do not think of this third option when we find ourselves in the throes of dryness. We look for ways to change it or to escape it, and these are certainly appropriate responses in many cases. Those are the first two options my friend mentioned. When they fail, however, we may not try to change how we view the situation, and this can be the key that enables us to see an unexpected way forward.

A simple example of this can be found in the story of a friend of mine who had put a lot of energy into making arrangements for a retreat. This was coming at an important transition in his life, and naturally he wanted everything to be perfect for himself and his companions. They would have a peaceful place in which to ponder the voice of God speaking in the depths of their hearts.

Imagine his dismay when he discovered that another group would be using the same facility – a group of girls and young women, whose activities were suitable for energetic children and adolescents, but which created more noise than my friend had been expecting. He ran the risk of being able to hear nothing of God but only the laughs and squeals of little girls.

As we talked about it, we came to see that he could try to think about changing his perception of the situation. After all, I suggested, if the noise had come from flocks of songbirds, it would have been noise but he would feel differently about it. What if instead of hearing noise, he tried to let it be music, the song of joy and delight of children, beloved of God and blessed by God's creation. He might have to hear something, but he could decide how he would hear it.

I admit this was a lesson I had learned from a similar experience I had at a retreat house in California. It was located on an old estate, once in the center of an orange grove on a hillside. Although it was not visible from the retreat center, an interstate highway had been constructed below the hill, and traffic streamed up and down the highway at all hours of the day and night, along with its concomitant noise. The noise was not deafening, but it was noticeable and for a while I let it annoy me. What a shame, I thought, that such a beautiful location had to be ruined by traffic noise!

As I grumbled in my mind, I began to think of better places to be on retreat, places near the ocean perhaps. There I would not have to listen to cars and trucks buzzing by, but I would be lulled by the noise of the waves. That's what a retreat house should have! Waves!

And then it hit me. I couldn't see the cars and trucks, and if I listened, the noise rose and fell. It was in fact not unlike the sound of waves. All I had to do was let the noise be what it was, and it could have been the waves on a beach as invisible to me as was that interstate.

It was a silly thought, perhaps. But I didn't waste any more time on that retreat fuming about car noises. I didn't have to let them drown out what I had come to hear: God in my heart.

In his profound teaching on the experience that has come to be called the dark night of the soul, John of the Cross helps the person experiencing this particular kind of spiritual dryness see the experience from a different perspective. He helps me see that God has not abandoned me, despite my feelings or my confusion, but that God is perhaps being present to me in a new way in the gift of contemplative prayer and union. This may be unfamiliar to me and seem to be regression, whereas, properly understood, it is in fact a sign of spiritual progress. It is a matter of changing my perspective so that I begin to see things from God's point of view.

A wonderful example of this can be seen in a famous painting of Salvador Dali, based on a drawing of the crucified Christ by John of the Cross. The original drawing, preserved in the museum at the Monastery of the Incarnation in Avila, intrigues the viewer because of the angle from which it is drawn. Most familiar views of the crucifixion are head-on or perhaps looking up at the figure of Jesus on the cross. John's drawing looks at the body from the side and a bit from above. It is such an unusual angle that the viewer's first impulse is to shift position or even to reach out and turn the drawing, trying to make it fit into the expected perspective. Dali's beautiful painting emphasizes this view from above, so that one is looking down, as it were, from heaven on the scene of Christ's death. At first, it may look like a bird's-eye view, but then the thought come: It is perhaps a God's-eye view.

If you read the accounts of the Passion in the four gospels, you cannot help being struck by the way the perspective in John differs from the perspective in the first three gospels. The story is the same, and we tend to merge details from each version into one continuous storyline in our imagination. Yet the Jesus in John seems to be moving in a different atmosphere than the same Jesus in Matthew, Mark and Luke. I would contend that it is not the story that is different, but the perspective. Matthew, Mark and Luke tell the story very much from the human point of view; John gives us a mystical glimpse into the same events with the eyes of God.

In the Dali painting, the bloody brutality that marks our ordinary perception of Calvary is missing, and instead there is an air of timelessness and even serenity. Instead of the walls of Jerusalem in the background, we see a boat beside a body of water, and nearby stands a figure in the uniform of the papal Swiss Guard. The mind is directed not to the past but to the future, to the action of God that will flow from this supreme act of love on the part of Jesus: the establishment of the church as the sacrament of his body and the instrument of the invitation to universal salvation.

When you and I stand on different sides of an image and look at it, we see the same object, but what we see is not the same. My view – and yours – is always partial. That is why we move around from side to side, walk around behind a statue or peer at a painting from different angles. Our view remains partial, but we seek to see more so that we may see more fully. We sometimes mistakenly think we have seen all there is to see. Dali's painting, like the original drawing of John of the Cross, is a reminder that there is more.

Dryness, therefore, can call us to change our way of seeing things, our way of seeing the world and ourselves so as to open out hearts and minds up to what Jesus calls "God's work." Dryness, tragedy and sorrow can be seen as an opportunity for grace more than as a sign of divine anger.

Of course, this is not to deny that sometimes our suffering is a result of our sinfulness, our selfishness, our falsehoods and our fears. In speaking of the dark night of the soul, John of the Cross notes that there are certain indications that point to the action of God. Without these signs, we may be dealing with the painful consequences of our actions. Yet even so, this becomes an occasion for repentance and for turning to God for healing and strength. Everything can be an opening for grace to the one who is seeking it.

My family originated in Wales, although the family later migrated to England and Ireland before making their way to the United States in the seventeenth and eighteenth centuries in several groups, some more identified with Wales and others with the Irish. The motto on the Welsh version of the family's crest is *In copia cautus*: "In time of plenty, be cautious." The flip side of that could well be, "In time of dryness, be open." What you think is a disaster may be the doorway to a treasure.

Chapter Three

Go Away from Here:
Detachment

A bird is as tied down by a thin thread as by a
heavy one; for no matter how thin it be, until it
be broken the bird cannot fly away.

> John of the Cross
> *The Ascent of Mount Carmel*

"My drug of choice is more," a friend once
said laughingly.

It was, however, not a joke. For so many
people in the modern world, certainly in so-called
First World nations, *more* is what we want. More
money to buy bigger houses to store more clothes to
wear to better restaurants to drink more exotic
wines. More, more, more. No matter how much we
have, it is not enough. It may be good, but it is still
not enough. All we want is more.

Remember when it was good enough to
have access to a telephone? Then we got mobile
phones. Then we wanted mobile phones that had a
more entertaining ringtone. And that would store all
our telephone numbers. (Quick! How many
telephone numbers can you recall from your own
memory these days?) And one that would show me
who was calling before I decided to answer. And
that would have a different ringtone for everyone
who called, so that I wouldn't have to look at the
screen to see if I wanted to answer. And one that

would play entire songs, not just a few notes for a ringtone. And that would let me send text messages. And that would let me read my email. And that would let me surf the internet. And that would run movies and television programs. And that would ...

And to think that William Shakespeare, Abraham Lincoln and Jane Austen all got along without even a land line!

With an economy based on consumerism, we have the strange phenomenon of a money-strapped government refunding tax money in hopes that people will rush out and buy more things. The solution to our problems is to buy! Some leaders of the United States actually told us that we had to keep shopping after the horror of 9/11 or else the terrorists would have won. At a time when the human capacity for caring for those hurt in a disaster was surging with a powerful force into the limelight, when the goodwill of the world reached out to us with an aching heart, we were told that the most powerful thing Americans could do *as Americans* was to continue to buy things. It was our fierce determination to return to the malls that would prove the resiliency of the values held dear by the people of this wounded nation.

Of course, similar absurdities could be found for most nations in most periods of history. My point is not that the United States is unusually bad, but that it is all too typical in mistaking material plenty or consumption of material goods for the highest human value. One reason that periods of dryness are so devastating is that they are periods when our emptiness is made so manifest that we cannot ignore it. We, who desire nothing so much as to be full, discover that we are empty. We have built leaking cisterns and they will not hold water.

We thirst.

It is as if we suddenly have awakened to the reality of our life. For some of us, that life may have been one of serious estrangement from the spiritual dimension, a life of sin in its most destructive and obvious manifestations. A life of selfishness, of lies, of hatred, of artificial loves, a life of emptiness, in fact. I have gone from satisfaction to satisfaction, but I am never satisfied. I am a gaping hole, a void, seeking everywhere to be filled – with material goods or frail human affection, finding momentary consolation in delicious food, in beautiful clothes, in McMansions. Yet somehow these have never been enough. So I have turned to friendships, which also may fail me; to love affairs, but an affair is an event, over and done, unable to satisfy the longing that constantly manifests itself as stronger, deeper, more urgent.

I may turn to alcohol or drugs to ease the ache. Yet each day I awaken to find that the pain and the emptiness are still there, at my core. I discover that no matter what I try, no matter how much *more* I get or use, I seem to grow emptier and emptier. The loudest voices and most persistent images that surround me assure me that the answer lies in brighter teeth, silkier hair, tighter abs and the latest fashions. I rush out to buy in order to deaden the voices of the terror that is within me. If I stop consuming, the terrorists will have won!

Then in the hard and unflattering light of some winter day in the soul, I wake up to the reality that as long as I keep this up, the terror within me has already won. These things have never worked, and *they will never work.* As the cliché (attributed to Einstein) goes, insanity is doing the same thing over and over and expecting a different result. The time has come to look for something else.

In the opening lines of his reflections on the first stanza of *The Spiritual Canticle*, John of the Cross describes such a person:

> The soul realizes what she must do;
> seeing that *life is brief* (John 14:5), that *the
> path to eternal life is narrow* (Matthew
> 7:14), that *the just are barely saved* (I Peter
> 4:8), that the things of this world are empty
> and false (Ecclesiastes 1:2), that *everything
> will end and disappear like spilled water* (II
> Samuel 14:14) ...

It is no wonder that the bride in John's poem calls out, "Where have you gone, beloved, and left me so unsatisfied?" Satisfaction is not to be found here.

So the voice of God says, "Leave here..."

The Carith story tells us that we will not find the life-giving water here, among these leaky cisterns. We must look somewhere else. Here is drought; here is emptiness; here is nothing. We must go somewhere else, somewhere Other. To reach a place we have never been, we must walk a path we have not yet taken.

"Turn eastward..." Turn away from the darkness towards the breaking light. Even though it may still be dark, it is in the east that the light will first appear. We must turn towards the coming light, turn even in the dark.

One of the most provocative verses in the Gospel of John is the first verse of chapter 20: "It was early on the first day of the week and still dark, when Mary of Magdala came to the tomb."

It was still dark.

Yet the resurrection had already occurred. Life had triumphed over death, but the Magdalene did not yet know it. Light had shone in the darkness of humanity's darkest night, but it was a light yet unseen and unrecognized. Mary had to go *in the dark* to the tomb. So must we turn towards the light that is coming while it is still dark in our hearts.

We must even, according to the mystical traditions of all the great religions, darken our hearts by turning away from the false lights of ephemeral worldly things, of distorted relationships, of abusive power. These pretend to be of the light, but they are not. We must let them go and walk away. To somewhere else, to somewhere yet unknown.

For a number of years I served on a committee that met in New Orleans every year during the last days before Mardi Gras. We attended a number of the parades and were told that to make a good Lent, one must make a good Mardi Gras. This struck me as a pretty transparent rationalization, until I began to reflect on what happens at a Mardi Gras parade.

I am not speaking, incidentally, of the sorts of things that the newscast likes to show, because the events we attended were family-friendly and fun, not scenes of drunken debauchery or exhibitionism. Still this is what I observed.

Most of the parades take place at night. People crowd the sidewalks; there is laughter and joking, jostling for position, merrymaking and the occasional excess. Then out of the dark one begins to hear music. The bands go by, the uniforms glittering, the batons twirling. Huge floats appear out of the darkness, kings and queens in gold and silver wearing bright jewels, lovely women, handsome men in masks. They fling coins and beads to the crowds. People reach for the baubles, stretching out their hands over the heads of children to grab things from the air. You pile the beaded necklaces around your neck and immediately scream for more. "Mister, throw me something!" You crawl on the ground to snatch at coins and stuff them into your pockets before jumping back into the fray.

More beads, more floats, more beautiful dresses and lovely masks, more coins rattling on the pavement. On and on it goes until finally it is over, and exhausted, you stumble home laughing, loaded down with your booty. What a fun night!

When you reach home, you look in the mirror and in the light what do you see? Cheap plastic beads. Colorful tin coins that will purchase no food, no shelter, no clothing. You lift the beads from your neck and suddenly realize how much they weigh. It is as if a burden has been lifted. The time has come for Ash Wednesday, the time to lay aside the false beauties of papier-mâché masks and plastic finery, the time to stop trampling other people to get things that sparkle in the dark but have no lasting value in the light. The time has come to be somewhere else.

It is very hard to let go. Especially when we do not see what is going to take the place of what we are releasing. Yet it is a fundamental law of the spirit. Some of the harshest words to be found in the mouth of Jesus – and therefore the most frequently ignored or spiritualized into meaninglessness – are his sayings about letting go.

"Follow me, and let the dead bury their dead." (Matthew 8:22; see also Luke 9:60)

"If anyone come to me without turning his back on his father and mother, his wife and his children, his brothers and sisters, indeed his very self, he cannot be my follower." (Luke 14:26; See also Matthew 10:34)

In a culture that often identifies religious values with strong family ties, these verses can be unsettling. Of course, at the time the gospels were written, circumstances may well have placed the believer in the position of choosing between her natural family and the faith family centered on Jesus. In a world in which one's personal identity was very much tied to one's family identity, this would have been a wrenching choice to face. Among the Romans, for example, even adult sons were under the legal control of their father until his death, at which time control passed to the eldest brother. To leave behind father and mother was tantamount to forgetting one's very self.

47

Detachment is hard for us because we have formed attachments to things or behaviors or people who have helped us cope with problems in the past. Just as it was hard for a first-century Jewish woman to turn her back on her father, or a Roman son to leave his behind, so it is hard for us to turn our back on the habitual sources of comfort and consolation that have sustained us: food, drink, gambling, gossip, unhealthy relationships.

The power of such attachments is sometimes spoken of today in terms of addiction. This term may be overextended and misused, but one cannot ignore the relative appropriateness of its application in many cases. There may be no addiction in a strictly clinical sense, yet the power of the attachment may still render a person virtually powerless in the fact of its object and make his life unmanageable.

And to get to another place, we must find another path.

John of the Cross is a poet of love, but most people, if they think of him at all, think of him in terms of suffering rather than rejoicing. If they have heard any of his lines, they will likely be not from *The Living Flame of Love*, but from *The Dark Night of the Soul*, a commentary, it is often forgotten, not about depression and pain but about a lover slipping away in the night for an encounter with the beloved. These famous lines etch themselves into the imagination, and, like the hard sayings of Jesus mentioned earlier, they are lines that most of us would rather skip over.

These lines are associated with another drawing of John of the Cross, a simple line drawing that represents the path up Mount Carmel. He made copies of the sketch for some of those who came to him for spiritual direction. The lines are also incorporated into chapter thirteen of The *Dark Night of the Soul*.

> To come to enjoy all,
> Desire joy in nothing;
> To come to possess all,
> Desire to possess nothing;
> In order to be all,
> Desire to be nothing;
> In order to come to know all,
> Desire to know nothing;
> To come to that which you do not enjoy,
> You must go by a way you do not enjoy;
> To come to that which you do not know,
> You must go by a path you do not know;
> To come to what you do not possess,
> You must go by a way you do not possess;
> To come to what you are not,
> You must go by a way you are not.

This sober, thoroughgoing and perhaps even frightening detachment is a characteristic theme in the teaching of John of the Cross. It elicits a visceral reaction much like that of the people who turned away from Jesus after hearing the Bread of Life discourse in John 6:60, saying, "This sort of talk is hard to endure! How can anyone take it seriously?"

No doubt there is an element of hyperbole in John's words, but that does not render them meaningless. It is to his life that we turn for a concrete example.

Due to a variety of circumstances and much confusion over ecclesiastical and civil jurisdiction, the young Carmelite reform movement begun by Teresa of Avila found itself in conflict with the larger Order of which it was a part. This conflict broke out into open persecution of some friars, and John of the Cross was the most famous victim. In December of 1577, he was seized by supporters of the opposition and held prisoner in the prison cell of the Carmelite monastery in Toledo for nine months.

The story of his suffering there and of his dramatic escape "one dark night" is worth telling, but the details need not detain us. In passing, I note that he himself spoke of this time as one of tremendous grace, an example of how one's perspective makes all the difference in one's experience.

After nine months in his cell, besides a pencil stub and some paper, John had nothing except a blanket and his tattered and filthy habit. This was all he had to protect himself from the cold and to shield himself from prying eyes. When the time came for him to escape, though, he had to tear the blanket up and, as though in a prophetic enactment of a Hollywood cliché, made it into a rope and let himself down out of a window. In order to escape, he had to tear up what seemed to be the only thing he had for protection. And, to underline the moral, when he got to the bottom, the makeshift rope was too short, and he had to let go of it and fall to the ground, just a short distance from a sharp drop into a ravine.

We too must sometimes leave behind what we thought was our protection our strength, that on which we relied in time of trial. When it no longer works for us, when it is no longer protection, when what had been the solution has become part of the problem, we must leave here, turn east towards the light, and go.

In his drawing of the path up Mount Carmel, John of the Cross sketched one path straight up the mountain to its top where dwelt the glory of God. To either side, though, he drew paths that went astray. One of them was the path of disordered desire for material goods, the goods of earth. The other path was that of disordered desire for the goods of heaven. For, he teaches, we can be led astray even by things that are good in themselves when we allow those things to hold us back from total surrender to God's will for us.

This can be hard to grasp, especially for religious people. We don't think of ourselves as being Pharisaical, but then, the Pharisees certainly did not think they were being hypocritical or that they were addicted to the forms of religion but not to the inner substance. The Pharisee in the Temple (Luke 18:9-14) was serious when he thanked God that he was not a robber, an adulterer or evildoer. No doubt he did fast twice a week and contributed his full tithe to the Temple, and thus in his intention, to God.

Yet we know that Jesus said he did not go home justified before God. We can do all the right things, as a brother told me once, for all the wrong reasons. When we do, we don't realize that our reasons are wrong.

Even when our reasons are good, though, even when the place we are in is holy and our companions are graced, we may be called to go elsewhere.

Some years ago I was attending a six-month renewal program on the east coast, and as usually happens in that sort of group, I became very close to a number of people. As the time came for me to return home, I began to wonder how I was going to deal with saying good-bye to these folks who had become such an important part of my life.

I remember one of the directors of the program had said to me one day, "These people have been the face of God for you." How could God want me to turn away from that face? Surely I was meant to stay with them.

A week or two before the program ended, we made a Day of Recollection at a nearby retreat center. We had been there a few times, and one of my favorite features was the large outdoor labyrinth on the property. I had walked it each time we were there, and found it centering and soothing. I had walked other labyrinths before, but this one was fairly large and made possible a longer walking reflection period.

This particular day during the break after lunch, I went out to the labyrinth. It was a beautiful June day, warm but with a slight breeze. I entered the labyrinth and began to make my way along the cobblestones. There were a number of us walking in the labyrinth, each at a slow but steady pace. After a few moments, I looked up and noticed that Brother Steve, one of the people I would miss the most, had just begun the walk. As we went around, I saw that at times the winding path had us walking almost side by side. At other times we were far apart, and at times we were on opposite sides of the outer circle, apparently walking in opposite directions.

Suddenly the lessons of the labyrinth dawned on me in a wholly new way. Steve and I and all the others on that labyrinth were all walking towards the same goal. Each of us was on the right path, but we were each where we needed to be on the path at that moment.

At times in life, we would walk side by side as we had done for the past few months. At other times we walk far apart. Brother Steve and I were almost the same age, but for fifty-two years of our lives, we hadn't known one another at all. The journey brought us close, and the journey would now be taking us to different places. Yet I could see that we would still be on the journey, we would still be sharing a path.

So I could walk on.

Sometimes the place we must leave is not a bad place, but a good one. We need to recognize that there may come a time when God calls us to put that behind us, too.

"Leave here …"

Chapter Four

The Wadi Carith:
Charity and Grace

What's love got to do with it?
Tina Turner

G. K. Chesterton wrote in 1910, "The Christian ideal has not been tried and found wanting; it has been found difficult and left untried."

As mentioned in the previous chapter, religious people, even sincere religious people, can be mistaken about the nature of the Christian ideal. Jerome Gratian, in a small work written in the form of a parody of the legislation for a religious community, speaks of those who are misled into thinking "that everything consists in doing many penances, or going about outwardly composed, or having much delight and consolation in prayer and other things that they imagine, all the while going around with a heart full of hatred, rancor and animosity, sinking little by little toward hell...""

The Christian ideal is charity, according to Jesus' response to the lawyer's question about which commandment is the greatest. Following up on Chesterton's remark, one might say that charity, therefore, has been much praised but seldom

---

* *Jerome Gratian: Treatise on Melancholy*, translated by Michael Dodd (CreateSpace, 2009) p. 59. Available through Amazon.com.

understood and even more seldom lived. When the Carith story tells us to hide ourselves in charity, what does it mean?

First off, the fact that the author of the *Book of the Institution of the First Monks* associates Carith with charity is one of the indications that the original was not in Greek, because the Carith-*caritas* connection works in Latin, indicating that the book was written in that language. The Greek word for love, as we usually understand it in the New Testament, is *agape*. But if we play with the word Carith, in true medieval manner, we do find a Greek word that connects with it, and that is *charis*, grace. So our reflections will play with both these ideas as we examine the sort of place in which the seeker is to place herself.

Much has been written about charity since Paul's famous passage in his letter to the Corinthians, and nothing perhaps has surpassed those words. Certainly nothing I can say will do so! I want only to offer a reflection based on my personal experience of charity, love, from the perspective of one who has received it.

Some years ago a woman who was on retreat complained to me that I kept talking about love and she had no idea what I meant by it. This startled me, because I knew that this was a supremely generous and self-sacrificing woman. I tried to point out the ways in which she herself was showing love, but she stopped me.

"I don't know what it means to be loved. You keep talking about God loving me, but I have no reference point for that. What does it feel like to be loved? What does *that* mean?"

So I pondered for a while my own experiences of being loved – by parents, by friends, by those who had been (or thought they had been) "in love" with me. As I did so, three common elements emerged, and I shared those with her. What follows is what being *loved* has been like for me.

First, acceptance. The people who loved me accepted me. They did not always understand me or necessarily approve of everything about me. My parents, for example, would have preferred that I go to college nearby instead of choosing to attend a university fifteen hundred miles from home. They were not pleased when I entered the Catholic Church while at that university, and they could not understand fully why I would choose to enter a monastery after graduation and forego having a family of my own. Yet in all of this, they accepted me. That was part of their love.

Second, challenge. Acceptance by itself can be pretty limp. If those who loved me just let me be, I would never have grown. Instead they challenged me to be better, to face my fears, to try new things. As a result I learned that I could stand up before a crowd and speak, that I could go to a foreign country and learn a new language, that I could even dance (more or less). I am learning now that I can write books. Part of the love those people had for me was the challenge to go beyond myself.

Third, and essential to my way of thinking, is commitment. Their acceptance and challenge became love when those who accepted and challenged me went further and stayed with me. They didn't just say, "Okay, this is who you are. This is how you can become better. Stay warm and well fed. Bye!" They walked with me, sometimes wept with me, sometimes helped me up and other times let me get up on my own. But they were there.

Acceptance, challenge, commitment. That was my experience of being loved, and those elements were present in all of the varied relationships that were worthy of the name love.

This story about my father illustrates all three.

When I was fourteen, I learned to drive while working for the summer on my grandfather's farm. An older cousin took me under his wing and taught me how to drive an old army surplus jeep. It was in less-than-perfect shape, and I had to learn to double shift and sort of slide into and through second gear. It had little pick-up, and I had to push the pedal to the metal to get it to move. By the end of the summer, though, I was managing well enough to feel confident as I looked forward to beginning my driver's education classes at school in September.

One day in the fall, before I had actually gotten into a car to drive in driver's education, my brother was playing down the road when dinnertime rolled around. My father tossed me his keys and told me to go get him. I made excuses, but he assured me I could do it. After all, it was a country road with little or no traffic, the distance to cover was only a block or so each way and I had learned to drive over the summer. Right?

I got into my father's 1957 Plymouth with some trepidation, but also with some excitement. After all, this was an automatic transmission. It even had what seemed like a sign of the future: the driver shifted gears by pushing buttons. I did not have to worry about the clutch or shifting gears with a stick. How hard could it be?

I started the engine, sat for a moment, pushed the button that put it into reverse and, as I had done many times with the jeep, floored the gas pedal.

Unlike the rickety old jeep, the Plymouth was in good shape and had approximately a gazillion horsepower engine. It flew out of the garage, narrowly missing my mother's car and the central supporting pillar, across the curve of the driveway and into a tree in our neighbor's yard.

I was physically unhurt – there is much to be said for the physical resiliency of a fourteen-year-old – but when I got out and saw the crushed rear fender, I was sick at my stomach. I waited for someone to come, but apparently no one had heard the crash that to me had seemed to shake the Texas countryside. There was nothing to do but go tell my father.

I went back into the house where he was still reading the newspaper and told him what had happened. He folded the paper, got up and said, "Let's go see."

We went out and he walked around the car. He jumped up and down on the bumper a couple of times and got it loose from the tree. Then he turned to me and said, "Get in."

Get in? Get back in the car? Surely you jest!

He was serious. He had me get back in the car, in the driver's seat. He got in and had me start the car, pull away from the tree and down the drive, and then he talked me through driving down the road to get my brother and all the way back. His only concession to my poor driving skills was that he let me get out and put the car back in the garage himself.

To me, that was a great act of love. My father accepted what I had done. I know he did not like it or approve of it. But he accepted it, and more importantly, he accepted me as the one responsible. He then challenged me to do better by having me get back in the car and drive. Finally, he committed himself to me by getting in the car with me, even though he saw what I had just done. That may have been the greatest act of love of all.

Accept. Challenge. Commit. Go and do likewise. Recognize, too, when love comes to you in this form. Our cultural expectation that love has to do with warm feelings may blind us to receiving it when it is offered in another guise.

To hide oneself in Carith is to place oneself in an attitude towards others that is charitable. It means that I must try to be accepting of others, that I must have the courage to challenge others and the strength to stick with them through the process. Under these circumstances, it is quite active.

It is, however, also to place oneself in *charis*, grace. And that is about an attitude of receiving. Not passivity, but receptivity. When I leave behind my former way of life and enter into *charis*, I enter upon a world that is pure gift. It would seem that such a thing would be easy, but it is not always easy for us to be in a mood or mode to receive. Receptivity builds on detachment. Having let go of what I clung to in the past, my hands are now empty to receive a new gift. But I may want only to get back what I left behind. I may have trouble seeing the new as any kind of gift at all.

We will return to this idea later when we discuss the ravens and the food they bring. For now I want only to underline how important it is to be open to what God sends.

Years ago, a novice told me that he had realized that his usual method of prayer was to repeat endlessly, "Listen, Lord. Your servant is speaking." I was impressed at his insight and at his humility in sharing it with the rest of us.

That made me think about my own approach to prayer, and I began to see that my prayer often consisted of giving God a To Do list. What I thought of as asking things from God was more a matter of telling God what to do, when to do it, to whom to do it and how. I even thought that God was not answering my "prayers" because God was not doing things my way and on my timeline.

For Carmelites, medieval and modern, the great model of prayer is Mary, the Mother of Jesus. As the one who most fully heard and kept the word of God, she exemplifies perfect discipleship. As the one who said, "Be it done to me as you will", she shows us the contemplative stance. And at the wedding feast at Cana, she shows us the power of intercession.

Go back and read the story of Cana at the beginning of John 2. You probably heard it read at the last wedding you attended, and you know the story. The bride and groom run out of wine, Mary goes and intercedes for them and Jesus, after some initial and obscure hesitation, turns the water into wine. Not only wine, but gallons and gallons of wine even better than what had been served before. The gospel writer says that this was the first sign Jesus worked and that, as a result, his followers believed him. We sometimes say that Jesus worked his first miracle in response to a request by his mother, and that is why we trust the power of her prayers for us today.

Yet is that exactly what happened? Go back and look at what Mary said in verse 3: "At a certain point the wine ran out, and Jesus' mother told him, 'They have no more wine.'"

She does not tell him to change water into wine. She doesn't tell him to do anything. His response to her implies that her remark contained a request, but the only people Mary tells to do anything are the servants, to whom she says, "Do whatever he tells you."

I agree with the tradition that sees this story as an example of the power of Mary's prayer, but the power lies in her utter surrender of the situation to Jesus and to his will. She does her part, she makes known a need. Then she steps back to see what he will do. Far from *my* kind of divine To Do list, Mary puts it all in God's hands. She knows what so many of us fail to grasp: There is a God, and it's not us.

In southeast Texas, the Trinity River periodically floods. There is a story that some years ago, when the river overflowed yet again, the sheriff's department sent out cars with loudspeakers to warn residents to be prepared to move to higher ground. As one deputy was driving along a dirt road, blaring his news, he noticed that most people immediately sprang into action and began loading up their vehicles. But one old man sat on his porch, rocking calmly away. The deputy pulled up front and yelled out the window to see if the old man needed help.

"Nope, son," the old man smiled. "God will take care of me."

So the deputy drove on.

A bit later, as the flood waters came closer to where the old man lived, an emergency vehicle from town came out to pick up stragglers. They drove by and saw the old man rocking away on his porch and called to offer him a ride.

"The water," they told him, "is rising fast."

"No, thanks," he called back. "God will take care of me."

So the emergency vehicle went on down the road.

A couple of hours later the road was flooded and as water was lapping at the edge of the man's house, a Red Cross boat came by. The volunteers inside called out to offer him a lift into town and safety, but he would have none of it.

"God will take care of me," he called from his soggy porch.

The boat motored away.

Soon the water had risen up into the house, then up the stairs and the old man was left sitting on his roof.

This time a National Guard helicopter came by and dropped a ladder down. A guardsman scrambled down the ladder and offered to hold it steady while the man climbed to safety.

But again the man refused.

"I told them others afore, sonny, and I'm telling you now. I don't need none of your help. God will take care of me."

And reluctantly the guardsman climbed back up to the copter and hauled up the ladder.

Later that night the water came over the house and the old man drowned.

After he spit all the water in his lungs out, he looked up and saw that he was standing at the gates of heaven, gazing on the loving face of God.

"God," he raged, "what is wrong with you? I told all them people you would take care of me! I had faith in you, but you didn't help me. You left me there to drown. What's the deal?"

God looked at him sadly and said, "John, I sent you a car, an ambulance, a boat and a helicopter. What more did you want me to do?"

The answer to our prayer may be right in front of us all the time. We just have to hide ourselves in *charis*, and let God choose the way to give what we need.

Chapter Five

Drink from the Stream:
Holy Spirit and the Power of Love

When the Spirit of truth comes, the Spirit will
lead you to complete truth.

John 16:13

When one thinks of birds in the Bible, it is
not ravens so much as doves that probably come to
mind: the dove that returned to the ark with an olive
branch in its beak and the Holy Spirit descending in
the form of a dove at the baptism of Jesus. Certainly
the iconography of the Holy Spirit has tended to
focus on dove imagery, although other biblical
images also exist and appear in Christian art. Some
of these may convey the mystery of the Spirit more
forcefully, particularly the complementary images of
water, wind and fire.

Fire certainly has its place in the Elijah
stories – the fire he calls down from heaven to
consume the sacrifice on Mount Carmel and the fire
that surrounded the horses and chariot that carried
him into heaven at the end of his life. His own
iconography often depicts him holding a fiery
sword, symbol of his zealous zeal for the Lord of
Hosts. Wind is also present, in the still breeze at the
mouth of the cave on Horeb in which the prophet
discerns the presence of God, and in that same fiery
whirlwind of his ascent.

65

While wind, water and fire seem quite different to us, they have certain qualities in common that make them great icons of the Holy Spirit. Not least of these is that, although they are palpable, there is a certain elusiveness to them. One cannot grasp the wind or fire, and water runs out of a clenched fist, though an open hand can cup it. Without water, breath or energy (fire), there is no life. Yet each can also be the bearer of death as a flood, a tornado or a conflagration. They are power, but they are not fully under human control. They come and go, they flow, they are mysteriously present yet constantly changing. One cannot step into the same river twice. We know not whence the wind comes nor where it goes. Flames disappear into the air, but the fire continue to dance and may even grow larger.

So the Spirit of God – present, mysterious, powerful but ungraspable, visible in effects though hidden in itself, dancing yet disappearing. How do we let ourselves breathe it in and out, how trust ourselves to lean into it and be blown by it, how let ourselves be warmed to life in its invisible flames? How, hidden away in Carith, do we drink from the spring? How do we live in the Spirit that flows there?

"To live with the Spirit of God is to be a listener," wrote the poet Jessica Powers (Sr. Miriam of the Holy Spirit). There is a discipline, even an asceticism to listening, not just sitting still and keeping your ears open. You can sit in a room with the radio on and not have it tuned to a station. Then you hear the meaningless static of the speaker, but can you say you are listening to anything? To listen to the radio means to tune in, to find a station, to get the volume set right, to turn off all the other machines in the room, shut the door to what is happening in the next room and across the hall.

Surely it means making some choices, too. I myself cannot listen to the radio and watch the television and read the newspaper and carry on a conversation all at the same time. If I try to do so, I can hardly claim to be listening or attending fully to what is being said or communicated by any of them. I have to choose one and let go of the others, at least for the moment.

In the spiritual life there is a certain asceticism to listening that is more general. You cannot read every spiritual book that comes out (not even all those written by Michael Dodd!); you cannot listen to every tape or CD; you cannot go to every lecture, watch every DVD, attend every retreat. You choose, you focus, you go for depth, even though this is sometimes at the expense of breadth. To try to get it all is to fall into what John of the Cross calls spiritual gluttony.

We may worry that we will miss something important, but the truth is that if we are listening for the Spirit, we will hear all that we need. We have to stop listening with our own ears in order to hear with the ears of God, for it is only in the ears of God that we will hear all things aright.

As we listen, so in a sense we gaze. At what? At mystery!

How much we want our listening and our gazing to produce clarity: clarity about what I should do, clarity about what my family or my community or my business should do. If only I could see and hear exactly what to do!

But living with the Spirit of God is not keeping a vigil of clarity so much as a vigil of mystery. Not mystery in the sense of something incomprehensible or something that is problematic; it is mystery in the sense of something always to be further understood, something further to unfold.

I recall some years ago a Jesuit wrote about an encounter with Mother Teresa of Calcutta, with whom he had gone to spend some time in India working in her house for the dying. He was a gifted man and was at a point in his life where he was trying to sort out his future direction.

After Mass his first day on location, he met Mother Teresa, and she asked what she could do for him.

"Pray for me," he said.

"And for what shall I pray?" she asked.

"Clarity," he promptly replied.

"No," she said.

He was startled and asked her to explain.

She told him that clarity was what he was clinging to and what he needed to let go.

"But you," he retorted, "always seem to have clarity about what you are doing!"

Mother Teresa laughed and said, "No, I never had clarity. What I have is trust. So I will pray that you have trust."

That is to live in the Spirit, within the mystery of God's care that is trustworthy. It is to attend to the unfolding of God's will, aware that this does not end today or tomorrow nor anytime or anywhere on earth. In a sense, the unfolding continues for eternity in the glory of heaven. So that is what we learn to do here in the darkness of faith: to keep the vigil of mystery in preparation for the time when we will keep watch in the glory of the Beatific Vision, something for which we have words but no clear idea. It is the same One that we attend, though there in Light and here in night.

Listening physically involves the ears and the eyes and even the entire body as we lean toward the speaker. When we hide ourselves in Carith, in the charity and grace of God, we lean towards the Spirit. We may be surprised to discover that this takes courage. There is a temptation to pull back from the strange stirrings of the Spirit, to fight the flow of the water rather than to give in and be swept away to we-know-not-where. To lean into the wind is to lean into an invisible support. One is upheld, but by what? To float in the stream is to be upheld by water, but one can also sink beneath the surface.

To lean into the wind, to float on the stream demands trust, trust that the Spirit will not let me fall flat on my face or let me slip beneath the waves.

That is one of the temptations that prevents us from making more progress: fear of falling on our face or spluttering with a mouth full of water, of looking foolish. I have to learn to lean into that wind with trust, to relax in that water, to let them support me and move me, take me somewhere, towards SomeOne.

In so many ways we are willing to surrender only if we know what will happen. I can endure the cross I have carefully selected or at least expected. It is the unexpected, the uncertain that I fear, and that I clothe in my imagination with terrifying and paralyzing forms that cause me to go rigid, unable to move or to be moved. When I am flexible and yielding like a tree in the breeze or a reed in the stream, I am safe. When I go rigid, I can snap and break in the wind or in the torrent. And then I do not move so much as fall.

The Annunciation story is a favorite biblical example of total surrender to the will of God. The Archangel Gabriel is sent by God to Mary to announce her blessedness in being chosen to bear the son of the Most High. Mary accepts, saying, "Behold, I am the servant of the Lord. Be it done to me according to your word." And the angel left her. (Luke 1:38)

What amazing words! *The angel left her.* The angel did not stay and tell her all the details about what would happen. He did not share stories about angels singing and shepherds and magi. He did not say that the son to be born to her would someday walk out of her home and wander the roads of Galilee and Judea and even despised Samaria. Or that she would someday walk a sorrowful road herself behind him as he carried a cross to a hill outside Jerusalem. The angel left her.

So in life for us. Even when we have those fleeting moments of certainty about what God's will is for us, we do not know the details. We do not know whether there will be shepherds or soldiers, whether there will be shouts of glory or of disdain. Like Mary, when we say yes, we do so in faith and trust. God's is the Spirit that blows us towards God, the stream that bears us towards life. Yet we do not know what we may see along the way.

Finally the one drinking from the stream and breathing the fresh breeze of the Spirit learns this great secret: the power of love to make anything a sacrament.

In the Catholic and Orthodox traditions, we speak of the seven great Sacraments of the Church, that is, seven ways in which we encounter God in Christ Jesus: baptism, confirmation (or chrismation), penance, Eucharist, marriage, holy orders and anointing of the sick. Each of these sacraments takes some created thing (water, bread, wine, oil, even human love and human contrition) and speaks a transforming word over it, so that the created thing becomes the instrument of our meeting God in a unique, sometimes unrepeatable way.

In the case of these officially recognized ecclesial Sacraments, the church regulates what created elements are liable to transformation. To baptize, one uses water, not tea or orange juice. To celebrate the Eucharist, one uses real bread and wine, not brownies and coffee. To marry there must be a sincere intention to be faithful to your spouse and an openness to your mutual union bringing new life into the world. Simply feeling warm towards each other and being willing to give it a try may satisfy civil requirements; it does not, however, make for a Sacramental marriage, which is a sign of God's absolute faithfulness to the covenant.

As for the sacrament of love to which I refer here – and which I call a sacrament by analogy to the seven ecclesial Sacraments, though it is not a Sacrament in the technical theological sense – , it does not matter over what you say the transforming word. You can speak love into suffering, you can

71

speak love over joy; you can speak it over coffee and brownies, over sweeping the corridor or paying the bills. You can speak love over standing in long lines at the supermarket or waiting for a traffic light to change. You can speak love over everything from the moment you rise in the morning until you lie down at night. You can even speak love over your sleep.

Two stories, set on opposite sides of the world, illustrate this.

First is one I read years ago in a devotional magazine, although I have forgotten where. It is the story of a woman who taught in a mission school in a village in Africa. As Christmas drew near, one of her students wanted to give her something special to show his gratitude for what she was teaching him. So he walked many miles to the ocean, picked over hundreds of sea shells until he found one that was whole and beautiful, and walked home with it in his pouch.

On Christmas Day, he shyly presented the shell to the teacher and, as she exclaimed over it, he explained where he had found it.

"It is beautiful," she told him warmly. "What a shame you had to walk so far to get it for me."

The boy looked at her, puzzled.

"Long walk," he explained, "part of gift."

It was, in fact, his long walk that made the shell more than a gift, that made it a sacrament of his love for her and all that she had given him.

The second story is set in the United States. Years ago in the small city where I grew up in East Texas, a young man entered the local state university. He was a fervent devotee of his own faith, and because he viewed Roman Catholicism in a very negative light, he announced to all and sundry that his personal goal for the year was to convince the local Catholic pastor of the error of his ways and to lead him to the light.

He began to visit the priest and to talk with him about the Bible and such things, and at the Easter Vigil that year, the young man was received into the Catholic Church.

A friend asked him, "What did Father Smith say that convinced you to become Catholic?"

And the new Catholic pondered it for a moment before responding, "You know, I don't think it was anything he said, really. He just loved me into it."

He just loved me into it. That does sound like what Jesus may have had in mind all along.

That we can love people into life means that we have been loved into life first ourselves. Through the instrumentality of others, we have been led to drink from the stream of the Spirit that flows from the heart of Jesus and springs up in the heart of the believer, a stream that unlike the one at Carith never runs dry.

The next chapter looks at some of those people.

Chapter Six

Ravens:
Unexpected Messengers of God

And these you shall have in abomination
among the birds, they shall not be eaten, they
are an abomination: the eagle, the vulture, the
osprey, the kite, the falcon according to its
kind, every raven according to its kind, the
ostrich, the nighthawk, the sea gull, the hawk
according to its kind, the owl, the cormorant,
the ibis, the water hen, the pelican, the carrion
vulture, the stork, the heron according to its
kind, the hoopoe, and the bat.

Leviticus 11:13-19

Ravens appear in various books of the Old
Testament, and there is a certain ambivalence about
their significance. As noted above, ravens as
scavengers contaminated by contact with death were
unclean.

(This raises the unpleasant question,
perhaps, of the nature of the meat they brought to
Elijah for his evening meal, although most readers
probably assume the meat was cooked in some way
by the same divine agency that provided it. There is
a rabbinic tradition that the ravens stole the food
from inns to bring to the prophet, but that creates
other problems.)

Ravens are not evil, for being unclean had to
do with ritual purity, not with morality. This is a

75

point that is sometimes misunderstood in cultures such as ours in which the notion of ritual impurity is unfamiliar. Except for Jewish and Muslim Americans, most of us in this country have no religious ideas about unclean food. We do have some cultural biases, however, such as a reluctance to eat certain kinds of meat. The notion of eating a dog or a grasshopper, for example, while having no religious significance, is repulsive to most of us. Yet there are places in the world where such animals are eaten and even considered a delicacy. In any case, we do not consider dogs or grasshoppers to be evil.

The raven appears in the story of Noah and the ark (Genesis 8:6-8), when the raven was sent forth before the dove to fly over the waters in search of land. The raven, no doubt finding ample carrion on which to feast, did not bother to return. Thus the raven was in a sense the first animal restored to the earth after the destruction caused by the flood. Still, the image of a dark bird hovering over scattered dead bodies is hardly as pleasant as that of a white dove flying over a renewed and pristine earth with an olive branch in its beak.

Although we tend to associate small and tender birds with scripture – the dove and sparrow, for example – ravens appear as examples of God's special care in Psalm 147:8 where the Lord is said to "cover the heavens with clouds, to provide the earth with rain, to produce fresh grass on the hillsides and the plants that are needed by man and woman, who gives food to their cattle and to the young ravens when they cry."

Everyone is familiar with the admonition of Jesus to consider the birds of the air, found in the Sermon on the Mount in Matthew (6:26), but Luke's version indicates that Jesus spoke specifically of ravens. (Luke 12:23) Note also that God feeds the ravens here as in Psalm 147. Apparently the carrion that sustains the ravens and that renders them unclean itself comes from God. Again we see that the idea of ritual impurity is not the same as immorality or evil.

In September of 1972, I went to the Discalced Carmelite novitiate outside Little Rock, Arkansas to be interviewed as a candidate. My conversations with the vocation director went well, but he told me that I would also need to meet with the novice director who had reservations about admitting me because I had been Catholic for only a couple of years. In the course of the interview the novice director, who was warm and charming, asked if I could deal with ambiguity. He later claimed that I had responded, "Maybe yes, maybe no." He thought I was trying to see if *he* could deal with ambiguity.

It is a vital question, however, that of our ability to cope with ambiguity. Contemplatives, as we will see in a later chapter, do not find their certitude in clear-cut answers but in God and God alone. So we cannot be certain that a messenger is from God based only on clear ideas about what such a messenger should look like according to our own lights. There is ambiguity.

God nourished Elijah by means of unclean ravens. In the Book of Numbers (22:28) we are told that God spoke to the prophet Balaam through the agency of an ass. God is not limited in the means of communication with us; we must strive to place no limits on our listening for that communication, however surprisingly it may come to us.

Here are some examples of how such communication can come if we are attentive.

A friend recently took a defensive driving course. He told me later that at the first class, the teacher said, "Don't let someone else drive your car."

"An odd admonition," I thought at first. As far as I knew, everyone in that particular class was there because of mistakes he or she had made driving, not because of letting someone else drive the car and mess up.

The instructor, of course, did not mean not to allow another person to use your car. His point was not to let other drivers, by tailgating or other reckless behavior of their own, so influence your driving that they force you to speed or otherwise drive foolishly. How often have I looked down while on the freeway to discover that I am more than ten miles over the posted speed limit, even though I am driving at the same pace as those around me? How often have I become angry at an aggressive driver and responded by driving aggressively myself? I have unthinkingly let someone else drive my car, or at least manipulate the way I am driving it.

The more I thought about the teacher's remark, the more I realized how applicable it is to non-driving situations.

There was a time in my life, not all that long ago, when I found myself fretting constantly over my employment, my very limited income, my lack of health insurance and other securities. One day, however, I realized I was letting other people drive my car – letting people who loved me and wanted the best for me make major decisions for me about what I would do for a living, how I would spend my time, what I was going to need to take care of myself. I was letting them set an agenda for an unknowable future that was having damaging effects on my present inner life. This was certainly not their intent, but that was what was happening. By letting them take the wheel from my own inner driver, I was headed for a spiritual and emotional wreck.

It is easy to let other people determine what matters most to us. As children, when our experience of the world is limited, we need parents, teachers and others to help us recognize what is important and what is not. This may happen when they point out that they cannot afford to buy us that must-have toy for Christmas, or that they do not want to buy us video games that focus on destruction and vengeance. As we mature, we are often grateful for the lessons that we learned and for the people who pointed us in good directions.

Yet as we mature, we also must assume responsibility for driving our own car, for making our own decisions, for living according to our own well-chosen spiritual principles. This idea came to me from an unexpected source, in fact, from someone who was not talking about my spiritual life at all, from someone who was teaching a course for people who needed to learn something about how to drive a car. Yet in the unexpected ways of God, he brought me bread for my day's journey.

Or what about the track coach?

Back in 1984, I was part of a wonderful year-long program in spiritual formation at St. Louis University. While there, we were able to take advantage of the facilities at a new recreation center, and although I am not the least bit athletically inclined, I decided to take the advice of all those people who suggested I would profit from regular exercise. One thing I did was take up jogging around the indoor track at the center. I plugged along, trying not to run out of breath or to give up too quickly. Most of those sharing the track with me were university students, fifteen to twenty years younger and in far better shape. Some of them seemed to fly around the track, but it was not the speed that caught my attention so much as the grace and smoothness of their movements. I bounced up and down, but these men and women kept a lovely stride and seemed to glide along.

I mentioned it to one of the teaching brothers in my class who happened to be a track coach.

"Most of those kids have that naturally," he told me. "I can tell the first day they come out, the way they move efficiently. They are practically tireless because their body is not fighting itself. It is something beautiful to see.

"But," he went on, "you can learn to run that way yourself if you try. Notice that they don't bounce up and down, jarring themselves with every step. You can break your bad habit of bounding" –

he had obviously seen me struggling around the track – "by taking your attention off the ground in front of you and looking at the horizon. Then try to keep the horizon steady as you run. If you can stay focused there, you will discover that over time you too begin to run without the jarring bounces. You won't tire yourself out, and you will come to enjoy running more."

Amazing. Just keep my eyes on the horizon. There is a verse in Isaiah that came to mind:

> Those who hope in the LORD
>   will renew their strength.
> They will soar on wings like eagles;
>
> they will run and not grow weary,
> they will walk and not be faint.
>   (40:31)

By keeping our eyes fixed on God, our spiritual horizon, we will find life less jarring, our own actions and decisions better and we will not grow faint or weary. And I heard that from a track coach who was trying to help me jog.

Another note on this story: Near the end of the thirty day retreat that completed the St. Louis program, I had a dream. In the dream I was running towards an unseen goal, but I was running gracefully and tirelessly. Alongside me ran my companions from the program, encouraging me and one another. We did not seem to be racing or competing. We ran just for the fun of it, something I seriously doubt that

I have ever done in real life. It was, nonetheless, a very consoling dream!

Perhaps one of the most interesting stories about an unexpected messenger from God is that of the founding of Alcoholics Anonymous. In 1934 a ruined Wall Street businessman named Bill Wilson, the victim of his own uncontrollable drinking, learned from a former drinking companion about a possible treatment for his alcoholism based on spiritual principles. While hospitalized, Wilson underwent an experience that convinced him of the reality of a higher power that was able to restore him to sobriety.

A year later while on a business trip he was sorely tempted to drink, and he searched out another alcoholic to see if spreading the message of hope might be of benefit to himself as well as to the man he met, Dr. Bob Smith. From their meeting developed what is now a worldwide fellowship of about two million men and women who follow a spiritual program based on twelve steps and who have found in them a way to recover their sobriety.

I note that the Twelve Step approach is not without its controversial aspects, although to date the basic approach has been applied with some success to everything from compulsive gambling and overeating to sexual problems. A friend told me of attending a continuing education program at her local Catholic university that was called "The Twelve Steps for Anyone Who Needs Them."

Now you may think that when I refer to unexpected messengers, I refer to those two drunken failures, Bill Wilson and Bob Smith, who discovered together a way out of the disaster of their own lives and a way to help others find freedom from a powerful addiction. Since the program itself is a spiritual one (not, AA members often point out, a religious one – at least, not in the sense of being allied with any specific religious tradition and with a precise definition or group understanding of what is meant by God or Higher Power), one might have expected a member of the clergy to have been the one to stumble upon it. Instead it was a couple of drunks, one a financial promoter and the other a washed up physician, who gave an impetus to what some people have called the greatest spiritual movement of the twentieth century.

The person I refer to, however, is neither Bill W. nor Dr. Bob, but Ebby Thacher – Bill Wilson's former drinking buddy and the man who showed up out of the blue with a personal story of recovery that changed Bill Wilson's life, and through him, the lives of millions of alcoholics and the friends and families of alcoholics around the world.

Ebby struggled with drinking for the rest of his life, unable to maintain his own sobriety, even with the personal help and care of Bill Wilson, the man whose life he had saved. It seems that part of Ebby's problem was his resentment at not having his own role in the creation of Alcoholics Anonymous more clearly recognized. He was a most imperfect messenger, and perhaps a bit like the prophet Jonah who grieved when his message to the people of Nineveh led them to change. Just as Jonah harbored a resentment, so Ebby did and resentments are a deadly luxury no one can afford. It is good to know that Ebby died sober in 1966, although the story of his last decades is not a happy one. Nevertheless, he was a messenger from God.

Wilson wrote in a book he gave to Ebby in 1960,

> Dear Ebby,
> No day passes that I do not remember that you brought me the message that saved me – and only God knows how many more.
> In affection, Bill

In Ebby's story, we see that the one who brings God's message may not be a perfect example of the content of that message. He or she may look to us like a failure in precisely the area under consideration. Like the ravens, they may appear unclean to us.

Before we leave them behind, I want to mention one more interesting little side note on the significance of the ravens. There are scholars who believe that the word in this story of Elijah at Carith that is translated as *ravens* may have originally meant *Arabs*. Some who support this reading do so because they want to avoid the unclean ravens, whereas others prefer it precisely because Elijah would have been fed by foreigners, just as he is in the following episode with the Phoenician woman. For the full impact, read the Elijah story and replace the word *ravens* with the word *Palestinians*.

How does that ring in your ears?

Jesus told stories about Samaritans and publicans, laid hands on lepers and corpses and performed miracles of healing for members of the despised Roman army that occupied his homeland and that openly worshipped idols in the Promised Land. A centurion who oversaw the execution of Jesus made a startling declaration of faith. Yet how many of the companions of Jesus found it hard to believe that God could use such as these to bring a word of salvation?

Even more amazing may be the fact that some people are evildoers. The tax collectors in first century Palestine did collaborate with the enemy. Some Samaritans did torment Jews passing through their cities. The centurion who declared that Jesus was the son of God may have been a brutal taskmaster. We have no way of knowing.

That does not mean that God cannot use such people to bring us a message we need to hear. And it does not mean that we see all there is to see in that messenger. Love, I used to tell the novices, is not blind. Love sees more.

John of the Cross said, "Do not think that because someone does not shine with the virtues you have in mind, that he or she is not precious in the eyes of God for what you are not thinking about."

And for our personal examen, he offers this: "What does it profit you to give God one thing if God is asking of you another? Consider what God wants and do that, for thus you will better satisfy your heart than with that to which you are inclined."

85

What does God require of us, the prophet Micah said, but to act justly, love mercy and walk humbly with our God? (6:8)

If we do that, who knows what ravens may bring us food? And who knows who may see us as the ravens in their lives?

Chapter Seven

Bread and Meat in the Morning: Meditation

"When you pray, say ..."
Matthew 6:9

A friend of mine describes his spiritual life in these terms: "I say one word when I get up in the morning – 'Help!' Two words when I go to bed at night – 'Thank you!'" In the next two chapters, we will look at ways to begin and end our days, ways that can incorporate the attitudes that underlie my friend's insight: a cry for help and an expression of gratitude.

In the Carith story, the ravens, those unexpected messengers and servants of God, bring the prophet bread and meat in the morning and bread and meat in the evening. First we will reflect on the morning food in terms of meditation.

Meditation can mean many things in many religious traditions, and sometimes the meanings seem mutually exclusive. We are not concerned here with definitions, however, so feel free to call what I will be describing meditation or anything else that works for you. My main concern is practice, not terminology. I grant that meditation as a concept incorporates far more than the practices I will be discussing, that these do not exhaust the possibilities and that these specific possibilities may not be the

87

best for everyone. In this matter, I follow Teresa of Avila who, when teaching her nuns how to pray, told them to do whatever most moved each of them to love.

John of the Cross says in *The Living Flame of Love*, "God leads each one along different paths so that hardly one spirit will be found like another in even half its method of procedure." (3,59) This remark comes as the saint is discussing the ways in which a spiritual director leads people astray as a result of believing that there is only one way to God, and naturally that must be the way that the director follows! Drawing on his wide knowledge of souls and his own profound experience of God, John teaches otherwise.

As mentioned in Chapter 3, John drew a famous sketch of Mount Carmel with three paths, two leading off to the side and the third ascending directly to the top. He did this to illustrate that people often go astray by following an illusory path of sensory or spiritual delight, failing to get to the top of the mountain, the dwelling of God, by the sure path of *Nada, nada, nada, nada*: Nothing, nothing, nothing, nothing -- but the will and the glory of God.

For me, the image of Mount Carmel has always represented as well John's teaching about different paths. There is one peak to a mountain, but there may be many ways up. Not all paths lead up, of course. Some lead to precipitous cliffs or to impassable thickets. Yet there are many approaches, often only visible once one has reached the top. Those who have ascended can look down and offer advice to others who follow them – and their advice may be not to follow the path that they themselves climbed. From a higher perspective, other paths may reveal themselves. One may even discover that almost any path will work, although some will require far more effort than others and present far more dangers. Any way up, though, is still a way up.

Having said that, and without implying that I have in any way scaled even the foothills, I want to offer three meditative practices that have been recommended by those who have gone before us up the mountain. I have found each of these useful at different points in my own journey, and I pass them on to you. They are not at all original, nor do they contain some hidden secret. They certainly do not exhaust the ways in which people meditate, and if you try them and do not find them helpful, try something else. These practices do, however, represent ways I have been able to taste the bread and meat of morning in order to gain strength for the day ahead. Each one is, in its own way, a confident call for help.

Also take note that a particular method of meditation that works well for a person at one time may not always be effective for them. The time may come to leave a particular method behind; the time may come when one will want to leave all method behind.

Lectio divina

First, there is the traditional method of prayer called *lectio divina*, or divine reading. This is historically associated with monastic spirituality, although it is readily adaptable to any state or mode of life. It appeals to many people today because it usually takes the form of reflecting on the sacred scriptures.

Because it follows a simple, natural pattern, it provides a structure to prayer that can be satisfying to those who like a clear method as well as those who need help restraining an easily distracted mind. On the other hand, the progression from step to step is so natural and simple that people who find structures confining will ordinarily feel no constraint at all. The process is spiritually so organic that, when it fits the one praying, it can flow gently with no apparent breaks from start to finish.

In its barest form, *lectio divina* consists of four steps or moments of prayer, which are called by the traditional monastic writers

- *lectio* (reading)
- *meditatio* (mediation)
- *oratio* (prayer)
- *contemplatio* (contemplation).

The *locus classicus* for this pattern is *The Ladder of Monks* by Guigo II, a twelfth century Carthusian, but it is found in this familiar form throughout much of the Christian spiritual tradition.

As Fr. Sam Anthony Morello points out in his wonderful little work, *Lectio Divina and the Practice of Teresian Prayer*, "Its elements are ingredients of a spiritual frame of mind, a holy discipline that intuitively and affectively dwells on a biblical text as a means of seeking communion with

Christ. The practice could also be described as dwelling on a scriptural text in the divine presence for the sake of radical change in Christ. Yet again, we could say that *lectio* is making one's own a small selection, phrase, or word of the Bible, in pursuit of greater faith, hope, and charity. In any event, *lectio divina* is prayer over the Scriptures."*

The ancient Rule of Saint Albert, followed by all Carmelites since the early thirteenth century, places this instruction at the core of their spiritual life: "pondering the Lord's law day and night and keeping watch at your prayers unless attending to some other duty." The allusion to the opening verses of Psalm 1 firmly points the pray-er toward the inspired word of God as the most fitting object of reflection. In the Christian world-view, the inspired word is ultimately rooted in the Eternal Word. So to ponder the law of God is to ponder God's complete revelation in the words of the Bible and most fully in the Word made Flesh in Jesus of Nazareth.

In a famous passage from his *Ascent of Mount Carmel* (22,3), John of the Cross points out the centrality of the Incarnate Word in all prayer.

> In giving to us the Son, who is God's
> one Word – having no other – God has

---

* Sam Anthony Morello, O.C.D. *Lectio Divina and the Practice of Teresian Prayer* (Washington, DC: ICS Publications, 1995). This is an excellent introduction to the theory and practice of *lectio*, based on the method of prayer St. Teresa taught to her nuns using the *Our Father*. Fr. Sam Anthony was the warm and charming novice director referred to in the story on page 75.

said everything together at one time in
this Word alone and has no more to say.

In context, this is part of John's explanation
for his caution about reliance on and expectation of
special revelations from God. In general, it is an
admonition that when we ponder the inspired word
of God in prayer, we always do so in light of the
Incarnate Word. By staying rooted in the life and
teaching of Jesus, we avoid being led astray by our
imagination or our purely human and imperfect
speculation. This will be important, as you will see
when I describe this simple method of prayer.

As we said, there are four parts to *lectio
divina:* reading a passage of scripture, meditating on
the passage read, praying over the fruit of the
meditation and contemplation. Let's look at each of
these very briefly.

Reading

First, reading. It is a good idea to select a
brief passage to begin. Some people will find a
gospel story or parable a good starting point. Others
may prefer a line or two from a favorite psalm. Still
others may want to select something from the
liturgical readings for the day, thus building a
relationship between personal prayer and the official
prayer of the church.

It is important, I say, to start with a brief
passage. Think of the ravens bringing bread and
meat to Elijah. They did not drop by with a huge
loaf and a side of beef that the prophet attempted to

gulp down in one swallow. Even at a rich banquet, we take small bites and chew carefully to savor the food. Otherwise we do not gain nourishment but indigestion. So it is with the word of God. Small bites, carefully chewed over and digested. That is the way to spiritual sustenance.

Ours is a culture that is inclined toward gobbling and gulping. You may have heard that the problem with instant gratification is that it takes too long. We want it all and we want it now, even in matters of the spirit. *Lectio* tells us to slow down, bite off only a bit, a verse or a phrase or even a single word. We are not in a competition to finish reading the Bible first. Instead we want to gain all that we can from each little bit before we leave it behind to take another bite.

One element of this way of reading is repetition. We read the verse or passage over and over. We read it slowly. We may want to read it aloud – as was indeed the ancient monastic custom. The one reading involved his whole body in the process, seeing the letters with his eyes, saying the words with his mouth and hearing them with his ears. I recommend that you try this yourself, although you may want to choose a private place to do so. You don't want to disturb people in the chapel by reading out loud!

Meditation

Reading in this way leads into the second step, meditating. We may believe that meditating is mainly an intellectual process in which we think about what we have read, and that is certainly an element of meditation. Depending on one's inclination and temperament, reading may lead to thinking about what you have read in a deliberative and reflective way, moving from point to point. Yet meditation need not only involve discursive thinking. It includes rumination, like a cow chewing its cud, turning the words and images over and over, just tasting them and looking at them, discovering meaning in an intuitive way.

If you are able to read aloud in private, you may want to try the following exercise. I will demonstrate with the opening lines of the familiar Our Father. Say the first line of the prayer: *Our Father who art in heaven.* Repeat that. Just say it the way you normally do.

Then say the line over and over, but keep emphasizing a different word.

OUR Father who art in heaven …
Our FATHER who art in heaven …
Our Father WHO art in heaven …
Our Father who ART …
Who art in heaven?
Our Father who art in HEAVEN …
In heaven …
Our …
Father …
Who art …
Our Father who art …
Father who art …

As you do this, you do not have to think about what you are saying, but you will discover that the same words keep opening up new levels of significance to you. These insight may lead you to further reflection and discursive meditation, but at some point you will move naturally into the third step in *lectio*, *oratio* or prayer as it is often understood.

Prayer

As a result of my meditation, I feel moved to praise God or to express sorrow for sin or to make a firm purpose of amendment or to ask for an increase in a particular virtue. This corresponds to what most people mean when they talk about praying, it is in a way my active part of the conversation which is *lectio divina*. In the first stage, I have attended to God speaking to me through the scriptures; in the second, God speaks in my own heart as the Spirit moves me to discover a personal application and meaning in what I have read. In the third stage I make my response in an affective manner appropriate to what has gone before. Of course, just as my meditation may have uncovered several layers of meaning and may have moved me in several ways, so my response may include more than one element. I may feel moved to thank God for the insight I have received, based on which I may want to express contrition for my sins and to promise to try to amend my life with God's help in some specific way. These things flow naturally from one another and weave in and out of this part of my prayer.

Contemplation

After this, I may want simply to rest in the presence of God in contemplation. This fourth step in the prayer does not necessarily imply a mystical state, although there may indeed be elements of such a grace within it. Rather it refers to the broader sense of contemplation, a simple loving gaze on the One who we know loves us, who is the Way, the Life, the Truth. We may find it easier to sustain this simple presence with God by slowly reciting a favorite prayer or psalm verse. I have always loved Psalm 27:4 for this purpose:

> *One thing I ask of the LORD,*
> *this is what I seek:*
> *that I may dwell in the house of the*
> *LORD*
> *all the days of my life,*
> *that I may gaze on the loveliness of*
> *the LORD*
> *And contemplate his temple.*

I have also found it helpful to repeat a line from a favorite hymn. In any case, it is useful to bring the process to a close in some way, even if it a simple recitation of a short memorized prayer such as the Our Father, Hail Mary of Glory Be.

In a given period of meditation, one may move through the steps several times or move back and forth among them. It is a simple way to pray and one with which most people quickly feel at ease.

Before moving on to the next practice, I want to remind you of the lesson in the last chapter: we do not know when and where and by what means God may choose to speak to us. While *lectio divina* refers first to a way of praying over scripture, it is a method that can be applied to other spiritual writings and even to things that may not be so obviously spiritual. By praying over the events of our day, over conversations we have had or things we have heard in the news, we broaden our listening to God and come to discover that God does indeed speak to us through unexpected messengers all the time. Everything speaks of God if we but learn to listen.

IF TODAY YOU HEAR GOD'S VOICE

The second meditative practice I want to share is one I learned in the novitiate, although I do not recall the exact circumstances. This is a practice oriented very explicitly to preparing for the coming day, and thus it is most fitting perhaps for an early morning meditation. It could, however, certainly be done the evening before as more remote preparation for the coming day, and this might prove particularly helpful if concern about the next day might interfere with sleep. This can be an excellent way of alleviating some of the stress.

In this method, I begin as always by placing myself in the presence of God and entering briefly into silence. I find it helpful to focus gently on my breathing, imagining that my own breath is a participation in the breathing of the Spirit of love in the Trinity. (There will be more on this in the next section.) Once I feel calm and centered, I begin to repeat this line from Psalm 97: "If today you hear God's voice, harden not your heart."

I repeat it slowly as I breath in and out, until the rhythm of my prayer matches the rhythm of my breath. There is no need to be in a hurry, but it should not take long to establish this pattern. Once I have done so, I begin to look over the coming day, continuing all the time to repeat my verse.

I think of what lies ahead of me, where I will be going first, whom will I meet, what I will do. Without forcing anything, I simply look at the day, all the while repeating my verse, and perhaps seeing how the events of the day and the people I meet may indeed speak to me with the voice of God. If I anticipate a difficult encounter, perhaps I imagine how the voice of God may speak to me words of calm at that time. I may imagine God speaking to me in the beauty of the countryside as I drive to work, or in the sight of children waiting for a bus. The prayer underlying my meditation is that I be open to however God may come to me this day.

I can recall one day returning from a meeting at a church on campus at the University of Chicago. As I walked back to the house, the leaves were falling and I passed a day care center where children were running to greet their parents who picked them up and hugged them. I was suddenly filled with gratitude for the beauty of the world and of life. I had certainly not included such a scene in my morning meditation, but I believe my morning practice had made me open to receive the grace of that moment in a way I might have missed otherwise.

Obviously, one can use this method in reverse, repeating the verse as you look back over your day to see where God may have spoken to you.

This simple practice, done for ten or fifteen minutes in the morning and the evening, could bracket your day and open it up to you in a way you had not previously imagined. "If today you hear God's voice, harden not your heart." Pretty simple, but it might change your life, one day at a time.

BREATH OF GOD

Finally, the third method of meditation I want to share is based on a Trinitarian theme, the breathing of the Holy Spirit. There is no need to go into details of Trinitarian theology here, but one traditional way of understanding the relationships of the three divine Persons of the Trinity is the foundation of this simple meditation.

In this way of understanding the Trinity, always affirming the unity of God, we consider how we tend to think of the Father, Son and Holy Spirit in their relationship to the world and how this reflects their inner reality, which is beyond human comprehension.* The Father we think of as the

---

* For the sake of simplicity, I use here the relational terms Father and Son with their corresponding pronouns, without implying anything about gender within God. It is a matter of faith that, no matter what words we apply to God, the reality completely transcends human categories

source of all that is, indeed not only the source of all creation but the source of the other Persons of the Trinity, although they are uncreated. The Father generates the Son, that is, pours out all that the Father is into the Son, except for being Father – that is, except for being the originator within the relationship. The Holy Spirit is said to proceed from the Father (and in the western church, from the Son) as in a breath of love. In the East, radical concern with the prerogative of the Father as source within the Trinity means that the Spirit is understood as proceeding only from the Father (though sometimes, it is affirmed, through the Son). In the west, it is generally held that one of the things given *by* the Father *to* the Son in the eternal generation of the Son is that the Spirit proceeds from the Son, too, but that the Spirit proceeds as from one source.

Try not to get a headache sorting that out, but follow along here, realizing that I am about to speak concretely of a reality that transcends even our notion of spirit.. The Father pours out all that the Father is (except for being Father) into the Son in generating the Son, who receives all (except for Fatherhood) as his own very being. The single bond of love that unites them is the Holy Spirit, the love that proceeds from them both as from a single source. All of this takes place in the single moment of eternity, not in a succession of moments. It simply IS.

---

of gender. I prefer in this instance not to resort to using "First Person" or "Creator" because these do not convey the relationship that I want to reference. All human language is inadequate even to most human mysteries; how much more so that is the case here

Knowing that in eternity this life of God IS, we can still imaginatively here in time and space enter into that life ourselves to some extent, seeking to place ourselves through God's grace in an attitude of total receptivity in preparation for the gift of communion with God.

This attitude of total receptivity, as it were, parallels that of the Son in the moment of his generation as indeed he receives all that he is from the Father, and as he returns in that same moment, in that very movement, the love of the Holy Spirit that the Father pours out to him so that he, the Son, might return it to the Father.

From this, the meditative exercise follows thus. I place myself in the presence of the Triune God and imagine the inner life of God: the Father pouring out all that it is to be God to the Son who is receiving all that it is to be God and the two of them pouring out the love that is the Holy Spirit rooted in God and binding all into one in a way beyond my imagining.

What I do in my meditation is place myself with the Son in receiving all that I am from the Father, especially insofar as I receive my human created reality as an image and likeness of God, thus conformed by God's power to the very Word of God, in whom and through whom all things were made and are held in being. As I receive all that, I am filled with the power of the love of God, which is the Holy Spirit, which I return in communion with the Son to the Father.

I attune myself to this through my breathing, breathing in all that I am, receiving all from the

101

Father, receiving it in communion with the Son to whom it unites me in returning all that I have received to the Father in the love that is the Holy Spirit. I breathe in God's gift, I rest in God's gift, I breathe out God's gift. Every breath I take is God's breath into me, every breath I exhale returns God's breath. I am immersed in the breath of God, the life of God, the Spirit of God like a fish in the sea. Breathe in, breathe out; receive life and love, return life and love. As simple as breathing, as steady as breathing, as necessary as breathing.

There are, of course, as many ways of meditating as there are people meditating. Both John of the Cross and Teresa of Avila insist on respect for the varied ways in which the Spirit of God leads individuals in prayer. These simple methods are included here not because they are the most perfect, but because I have found them helpful myself. You may find them helpful. If not, I am sure you will find your own way if you seek it diligently.

Whatever way you do follow, however, I encourage you to follow it regularly. The longest journey, as we all know, begins with a single step. It does not, however, consist of only one step. Through meditation, we discover what step to take next on the journey. For the journey to continue towards it goal, we must keep taking that next step.

Chapter Eight

Bread and Meat at Night: Contemplation

> Some time later the brook dried up because
> there had been no rain in the land.
>
> I Kings 17:7

When I was a student in Washington, DC, I recall at the Easter Vigil one year the homilist pointed out that the wonderful story of the crossing of the Red Sea did not end with Moses and the people looking back at Pharaoh's destroyed army and with Miriam and the women dancing as they sang the Lord's praises. After all that, they had to turn around and look out over the desert that still lay between them and the Land of the Promises. Forty years of wandering would have to pass before their descendants would cross over the River Jordan.

One disadvantage to reading the scriptures in small bits and pieces, the way it comes to us for example in the celebration of the liturgy or in the common form of Bible stories, is that we often miss an important point that comes in the next verse or the next episode.

Thus, in the account of Elijah's sojourn at Carith, drinking from the brook and fed by ravens morning and evening, we may not notice that this doesn't last. The brook dries up. What then?

103

When one has been practicing prayer for some time, it often happens that what had been nourishing and inspiring begins to lose its savor. The biblical passages that once kept opening new insights and filling your heart and mind with warmth and light no longer do so. Favorite parables and psalms no longer move you. There was a time when I could easily spend an hour pondering Psalm 27. Then, one day, that ease disappeared. This experience is not unique. St Teresa said that at one point she could read the entire Passion without shedding a tear.

The dryness that had been part of life's pattern before you began to pray seems to have returned. You may even begin to wonder if the spiritual experiences that had sustained you during the interval were illusions. The light of day is passing, night is coming. And in the darkness – what?

The ravens bring food to Elijah in the morning light and as evening darkness falls. In the Carmelite tradition, this can be looked upon as a sign of two moments in the spiritual journey, or two seasons. The first moment is the one that takes place in the morning, when our meditation and reflections lead us to enter into the challenges of the day through our own efforts, strengthened of course by God's grace and light. The second moment is the one in which our own efforts matter less and all is gift from God, something not achieved but received. We talk about these in terms of meditation and contemplation.

Meditation and contemplation go together, and the words are sometimes used interchangeably.

Here I follow that part of the Christian tradition in which meditation refers to prayerful human activity and contemplation refers to the human experience of being acted upon by God. Ignatius of Loyola speaks of "consolation without previous cause," indicating that the experience is not the direct result of our actions prior to it, but that it comes upon us as a gift bestowed by the sheer grace of God. This does not mean that contemplation is unrelated to our actions or lifestyle, but in the sense used here, the contemplative experience itself is not *caused* or manufactured in some way by my actions.

Although contemplative prayer is sometimes described as *passive prayer* to distinguish it from active discursive meditation, I suspect that this term may not express for today's readers all that it meant for writers who used it in the past. We tend to think of passivity in terms of weakness or listlessness or even as lifelessness. Contemplative prayer is far from lifeless! It is rather an experience of being filled with the divine life. We describe it as passive only in the above sense, that it is not something I produce through my own thoughts and actions.

Teresa, in the *Book of Her Life*, uses the image of four ways of watering a garden to describe methods of prayer typical of various stages of the spiritual life. The first three ways involve some work on the part of the gardener, each requiring less effort, but in the final method, water comes down as rain from above. The gardener does not have to produce it; gardener and garden receive it as gift.

This use of all of these terms – meditation, contemplation, active and passive prayer -- is not the same in every spiritual tradition, not even in every Christian spiritual tradition. The terminology is not as important as the reality experienced by all these thinkers and writers, that there are times when we lift the water from the brook to our mouths in our cupped hand, and times when the water is poured into our mouths. Or, in the image Jesus uses in John 7:38: "Out of the believer's heart will flow streams of living water." From the very depths of one's being, where God resides, flows the life-giving stream. It is no longer flowing from outside in, but from inside out, from God's own presence. This may seem to be different from Teresa's image of rain, but both are imperfect metaphors for a reality that transcends all images.

In this chapter, however, I do not intend to focus primarily on the more mystical aspects of contemplative prayer. The church herself turns to Teresa and John of the Cross for profound teaching on these matters, and their writings are happily readily available in good modern translations and with exemplary commentaries.*

Instead I want to talk about contemplation more in terms of the more ordinary meaning of the word: to look thoughtfully and attentively, to gaze, to ponder. This also fits the food the ravens bring in the evening, when the time for effort is over and the time to rest – even in the dark – has come upon us.

---

* I recommend the American English translations and studies that are provided by ICS Publications, 2131 Lincoln Road NE, Washington, DC 20002-1199. They can be found online at www.icspublications.org. For the sake of full disclosure, I admit happily that I am a former member of the Institute of Carmelite, whose publishing arm is ICS Publications.

The temptation in the darkness is to work harder. What is needed is to rest and let God send the gifts of eventide. We might think of sitting around a camp fire in the evening, gazing, seeing nothing specific perhaps, but seeing nonetheless in a different and more profound way. We no longer see the logs, but we see the energy contained within the wood becoming light and warmth.

This is the sense of contemplation already mentioned above in our description of the final stage of *lectio divina*: a simple loving gaze on the One who we know loves us, who is the Way, the Life, the Truth. John of the Cross speaks of the loving awareness of God. It is similar to the experience that results from our awareness and appreciation of the beautiful. Beauty is given to me, comes upon me, reveals itself to me. Some forms of beauty require an attentive and educated eye or ear, yet even so, the beauty comes to the beholder, the listener.

In the Fourth Dwelling Places of her masterwork, *The Interior Castle*, Teresa speaks of the person who has begun to move from the earlier stages of active prayer and who starts to experience habitual contemplative prayer. Although the Fourth Dwelling Places marks the transition to mystical prayer, Teresa recognizes that this does not mean that everyone experiences a clear and distinct break. Recalling again her appreciation of the unique way the Spirit guides the individual, Teresa knows that her schema is an approximation. Yet she believes that most of those who give themselves to the practice of prayer seriously for some time and who predispose themselves to simpler forms of prayer will come to know this simple experience that she calls the prayer of recollection. It may include some activity of the understanding or not, but the primary element is inner quiet in the presence of a loving God.

What is the object of contemplation, then? The ravens bring Elijah bread and meat. To the medieval imagination, this calls to mind the object of all contemplation: the Bread come down from heaven, the Word made Flesh. In the Teresian school of spirituality, the Incarnate Word, what Teresa calls the Sacred Humanity, will always be at the core of prayer. Critics sometimes accuse John of the Cross of lacking Teresa's Christocentric emphasis, but he too places the focus on the Word in his own way.

Some years ago when I was visiting my parents, my young niece was there wearing a woven anklet with the initials *WWJD* on it. I asked her if she knew what they stood for.

"What would Jesus do?" she replied promptly, smiling up into my face. Then she looked down at the anklet for a moment and turned a puzzled look on me. "What does that mean?" she asked.

Obviously the anklet was more a fashion statement than a religious statement for her at that age. The question she asked, however, was a profound one: What does it mean to ask what Jesus would do?

I suspect some of the people behind the marketing of WWJD jewelry and accessories may have only been asking how much they could make financially, but behind it no doubt lay a sincere wish to find a simple way of calling people – young people, in particular – to reflect on their behavior in the light of the behavior of Jesus.

In this, they were continuing the tradition found all the way back in Paul's first letter to the Corinthians: "Imitate me, as I imitate Christ." (I Cor. 11:1) In other places, the context makes clear that imitation of Christ is also meant: "Become imitators of us and of the Lord." (I Thess. 1:6); "Therefore be imitators of God." (Eph. 5:1) And, of course, one of history's most popular books of Christian devotion bears the very title *The Imitation of Christ.*

John of the Cross, accused as I mentioned earlier of lacking this Christ-centered sensitivity, nonetheless in his *Ascent of Mount Carmel*, offers this advice to the person seeking union with God:

> First, have habitual desire to imitate Christ in all your deeds by bringing your life into conformity with his. You must then study his life in order to know how to imitate him and behave in all events as he would.

> *Ascent of Mount Carmel* I,13, 3

I would like to point out something that may be easy for believers to overlook in this advice. John says we "must study his life in order to know how to imitate him and behave in all events as he would." That seems straightforward and points us toward the Gospels, the word of God that we discussed above in

109

the section on *lectio divina*. And clearly we must turn to the Gospels as our primary source for understanding the life of Jesus.

Yet there is a danger that we need to beware. Sometimes we unconsciously fall into the error of thinking that the Word did not become *flesh* so much as that the Word became *text*. We do not turn our gaze upon the living person of Jesus but upon the text of scripture. And we easily think that the particular translation that we have before us or that we prefer is the fullness of the word of God.

It is not so simple. There is an Eastern story about the spiritual master warning his disciples not to mistake the finger pointing at the moon for the moon itself. Even the inspired text points beyond itself.

John of the Cross talks about focusing on the life of Jesus. To me, this means that we gaze upon the living Jesus, not the words *about* Jesus. God's Word became flesh, not text. When we focus only on the words *about* Jesus we can let ourselves be led astray. If you think I exaggerate, reflect on the tragic divisions within the Christian community that are due to different interpretations of biblical texts. We need to contemplate what Jesus did and learn the lessons contained in his example.

So What Would Jesus *DO*?

This approach to prayer is perhaps more commonly associated with Ignatius Loyola and the Society of Jesus. The *Spiritual Exercises* of St. Ignatius, which were familiar to both Teresa of Avila and John of the Cross, were built around this kind of contemplation of gospel scenes into which one imaginatively enters, with special attention to the sensory details of the scene to render it more realistic and engaging.

This method of prayer is not mystical or infused contemplation in the technical sense of the word, but it is a form of simply gazing on truth in love. For nearly half a millennium, the followers of Ignatius have demonstrated the transforming power of such a gaze. The goal of the exercise is not to gain information but to be converted. Salvation, not information, is the key. It is too look beyond the wood to see the fire.

This way of praying can be part of the active meditation that we discussed in the last chapter. When one habitually prays in this way, it can lead to feelings of conviction and determination and other acts of will. It can be part of the delight of prayer. And to the degree that it is part of that phase of the spiritual journey, it too can eventually dry up. I may discover that I can no longer employ my imagination in the same way, I am no longer able to create an interior Cecil B. DeMille spectacular. When the stream dries up, then what?

This is when contemplation moves into the darkness, but a darkness that still has a Person at its center. At this point, my eyes must come to rest on Christ crucified and the great mystery therein. When the delights no longer delight, when the answers no longer fit, when the world turns upside down, where else can we go? To the cross of Jesus, there to stand, sit or kneel and simply look on truth and love. To look through the wood of the cross and into the powerful yet elusive fire of the Spirit. And let the Spirit of Truth and of Love transform us.

Part of the truth of love is that life remains a mystery. Unlike the story of Abraham and Isaac on the mountain, there will be times when, to borrow a powerful line from Jessica Powers, "alas, alas, no angel came."* Like the Jesuit who met Mother Teresa, we hope we will find clarity. What we find, with God's grace, is trust, but trust in the dark.

Is that it? Are we to be left at the foot of the cross, trusting but stunned and empty? On the human level, this may seem so. Yet there are those – people like John and Teresa, Ignatius, Catherine and Francis and Clare – who report that there is more. As for that, I have only a story.

Outside Milwaukee there is a beautiful church, the Basilica National Shrine of Mary, Help of Christians, popularly known simply as Holy Hill. Set in the rolling hills of the Kettle Moraine, a wonderful landscape sculpted by glaciers, the church and its spires can be seen from many miles. Up to three quarters of a million people visit every year, and many of them climb to the top of one of the spires, the observation tower.

It is 178 steps, beginning in a dark little lobby at the base of the church, proceeding up through a rather narrow stairway for a couple of

---

* "Take Your Only Son", *Selected Poetry of Jessica Powers* edited by Regina Siegfried and Robert Morneau (Washington, DC: ICS Publications) 1999, p.153.

flights with only room for one person to pass, which makes for major traffic jams during the busy season – then up through several more flights of stairs where you are completely enclosed, then past a level where large round windows let you catch a glimpse of the world outside and then up a few more flights until finally you come to the uppermost platform, 1800 feet above sea level. On a bright clear day you can see Lake Michigan and dozens of smaller lakes scattered around the Kettle Moraine. It is a glorious sight in any direction and well worth the climb.

But during the climb you are not aware of how beautiful it is outside: mostly you are aware of the stairs you have to climb, the shoes of the person ahead of you, the ache in your leg at a certain point when you wish you had been counting so you would know how many steps are left. But then that last step and you move out into the light.

That climb is in many ways analogous to our spiritual lives. We begin pretty much in the dark and we probably don't know which way to go, but there is only one way so we head up. We begin to pray. It can be kind of fun at first, you have a lot of energy and take a couple of steps at a time as young people are wont to do. And in the beginning there is only room for one person, for me. I am closed in on all sides by my concerns, my likes and dislikes, my self. My prayer is largely about myself. Even when I bring others into my prayer, they tend to be people with close connections to myself and I intercede for them. Or they are people I have difficulty with and I pray for the grace to deal with them. More likely in the beginning, I pray that they will change.

If I am in community I probably think that I could make progress a bit faster, in fact, if some of these slowpokes ahead of me would get out of the way and stop blocking me. At some point in here I realize that I have stopped taking the steps two at a time.

But I keep climbing and the corridor widens out. There is room for traffic to move in both directions, I learn not to hog the stairs, to let others have their passage. I find I am able to breathe a bit better. I begin to look around now, not as absorbed with myself, but I don't see very much. The walls are bare, an occasional bit of graffiti perhaps to indicate that someone has been here before. And I hear other people laughing and talking, some on their way back are chatting about how wonderful the view is. It sounds good, but I don't see anything except these stairs.

And I begin to wonder exactly how many levels is this? How far have I come? How far do I have to go? Do I really want to do this? After all, there is a large observation platform out in front of the church, no climbing, no pushing, not a bad view, really. Perhaps I should have been satisfied with that.

But if I persevere, I come to a place where I get a glimpse of the view, suddenly there is an opening and I can see trees below and flashes of light, I begin to sense what those who went before me are talking about. Now this is good! I think I will stop here for a while, so I do. I step away from the stairs and peer out the windows and relax. I may even tell myself I have arrived at spiritual maturity. After all, my perspective is much better here, I see

114

more, the air is cleaner, and I am away from the noise down on the platform.

But after a while I will notice that there is still a roof over my head that some people are going and coming on that ladder, that apparently there is more to see.

Well, I can do that, I tell myself.

So I get back on the ladder and head up. But to my dismay, as soon as I get to the next level, I am back in the dark. I thought the view would be continuous now, I thought it would just get better and better. Instead it feels like I have slipped back, back to the earlier darker stairwell. It is not so crowded but it is not pleasant either. I liked it better where I first stopped to look.

Maybe I should go back? Maybe that was where I was supposed to be. Maybe this stairwell is an illusion or a dead end. Surely once I come into the light I cannot expect to go back into the dark, once I find prayer satisfying I will never be faced with dryness and distraction again. Once I have seen the view, must I let it go? Maybe even that view was an illusion. Maybe this climb is all there is. My calves are beginning to hurt, too. Why didn't I count the steps?

And then unexpectedly SomeOne reaches down through an opening and lifts me up. And there I am, on the top, with a view of a thousand acres of light. And the 178 steps are forgotten, the partial view of my earlier resting fades away. And I look out to the horizon where my eyes fail but my heart can see forever. I discover that there is a greater reality than the confines of the tower and its stairs.

The world is bigger and more beautiful than that. So much more.

That climb can represent many journeys we make. It may represent the ascent from ignorance to the first light of faith. It may represent the long discernment of a vocation. It may represent at another level the whole journey of my life. We often feel ourselves hemmed in, caught on stairs that may seem to go nowhere, without anything but the echoes of other travelers to tell us what lies ahead. We are often tempted to go back.

One of the fascinating psychological mechanisms that operate within us is called regression: when confronted with a new challenge, we tend to go back to behaviors that calmed us down before, even when those behaviors are no longer appropriate. The desire to climb back down the ladder to where we first caught a glimpse of a light; or even to climb all the way back down into the dark lobby where we see nothing and are curled in upon ourselves like a fetus in the womb. But life, vocation, prayer all call us upward.

And that call to move can be a consolation just as it is a challenge. A Carmelite told me once that the only thing that got him through some rough spots as a postulant, the initial stage of his religious training, was the awareness that no one has a vocation to be a postulant, that is, God doesn't call anyone to stay there. At those times when we are pretty self-satisfied and complacent, the call to move onward can be a nuisance; when we are unhappy, it may be a relief.

There are many, St. Teresa says, who remain at the foot of the mountain because they lack courage. A very determined determination is what she wanted for her daughters and her sons and any who would follow her. But she promises if we stay with the climb, we will come out onto the ledge of light. More accurately, we will *be brought* out onto the top of the mountain where John of the Cross says nothing can be found but the glory of God. When we get there we will know that it is pure gift, that our climbing has played its role, but what we receive at the end is not what we have accomplished but what God has given – God's very self, boundless and sweet, an infinity in which to rejoice.

Which brings me to my final point about contemplation at the end of the day: gratitude. Recall my friend's final words each day – Thank you! This is the best way to end the day, the best way to end any journey: saying thank you.

The Liturgy of the Hours, the church's prayer by which she consecrates each part of the day to God in prayer, begins the day with praise and ends the day with intercession and gratitude. Vespers is a time not only to ask again for help through tonight, it is time to express our thanks for al the blessings that have come our way.

Some of us find it hard to express gratitude for all the things that have come our way. Yet the contemplative comes to know gratitude for it all, even the dark and confusing bits.

Which brings me to my final story.

When I was a student in Washington, DC, I was blessed to have a wise and experienced Carmelite as my spiritual director. At one point, I went to him in much confusion and sorrow as I

117

struggled with a situation that I did not know how to handle. After some discussion, much of which centered on my need to accept things that I could not change, he sent me home with this instruction: "Take fifteen minutes of your prayer time this evening thanking God for this situation in your life."

I assure you that it struck me as the most foolish advice I had ever been given! But I went home and did it.

I began to thank God. At first it was hard not to drift into complaining, but I stuck to it. Gradually I began to discover hidden blessings in that situation, things I had overlooked before or discounted. And then, I began to see that it was not a merely tolerable situation; but it was a great gift that had enriched my life already in unexpected and unappreciated ways. Even more, it would continue to do so if I would open myself to receive the gift.

That fifteen minutes changed my life.

At the end of every day, look back and give thanks. Thanks for the obvious blessings, thanks for the small and the large, thanks especially for the hidden ones. They may be the ones brought by ravens, the nourishment you need most of all.

Epilogue

We come now to the end of this reflection this somewhat rambling gaze at a long-ago tale, of a man in a cave by a spring, fed by birds. It was not the end of his story, nor is this the end of the reflections that the story calls forth.

One thing that my reflections in the Carmelite mode have taught me is that the truth is always bigger, and that love always sees more.

May your vision grow ever greater.

See, I will send you the prophet Elijah before that great and dreadful day of the LORD comes. He will turn the hearts of the parents to their children, and the hearts of the children to their parents ...

Malachi 4:5-6

Appendix 1
Summary of Biblical Elijah Stories

As I mentioned in Chapter Eight, there is a disadvantage to our custom of reading or hearing the biblical stories as if each unit were complete in itself and not part of a longer narrative. Although in some cases this may be true, we can gain new perspectives by reading an entire story at one sitting. For example, try to read the Gospel of Mark at a single sitting. It is not very long, and you may begin to notice connections between events that had escaped your attention before.

The method I have followed in reflecting on the story of Elijah and the ravens at Carith certainly is susceptible to this sort of distortion. One reason I added the final chapter, reflecting on the fact that the brook ran dry, was to show that the meaning of God overflows the stories beyond where we place limits, sometimes quite literally into the next verses.

The Elijah story does not end at Carith, nor at his triumph on Mount Carmel or with the encounter at mouth of the cave at Horeb. Some parts of the Elijah cycle are hard for us to fathom. We may rejoice to see fire come down to consume the sacrifice at Carmel, but what of the fire that descends to consume the fifty soldiers who had been detailed to accompany Ahaziah's captain to call Elijah to the court? We can at least understand that the 450 prophets of Baal who were slaughtered at Elijah's command after the victory at Carmel were servants of a false god. Yet that is a part of the story we may prefer to skim over.

Yet I believe there is something of value for us to learn by reading the whole story, and by reading it more or less straight through. My own sense is that only by reading the scriptures without skipping the parts that make us uncomfortable, can we begin to understand how to read the scriptures in order to hear the revelation of God as it unfolded and as it unfolds.

I encourage you, therefore, to read the Elijah cycle in its fullness. As you do so, reflect on the parts that inspire you and the parts that agitate you. Both, I suspect, are messengers to you.

Ravens, perhaps?

This is a summary of the Elijah cycle as found in I and II Kings. Elijah is also mentioned in later chapters of II Kings in the stories about Elisha, but they do not add to the story. Although there is reference to Elijah in II Chronicles 21, it is not part of the Elijah-Elisha cycle, being apparently an instance of attaching the name of an important prophet of the past to a letter from a different time and place.

1. Elijah confronts Ahab – I Kings 17:1
2. Elijah at Carith – I Kings 17:2-7
3. Elijah and the widow of Zarephath – I Kings 17:8-24
   Miracle of the flour and oil
   Raising of the widow's son from the dead

Appendix 2
Elijah in the New Testament

Elijah appears by name in the following passages of the New Testament.

Mathew 11:14
Matthew 16:14 (Mark 8:28, Luke 9:19)
Matthew 17:3-4 (Mark 9:4-5, Luke 9:30-33)
Matthew 17:10-12 (Mark 9:11-13
Mathew 27:47-49 (Mark 15:35-36

Mark 6:15
Mark 8:28
Mark 9:4-5
Mark 9:11-13
Mark 15:35-36

Luke 1:17
Luke 4:25-26
Luke 9:8
Luke 9:19
Luke 9:30-33

John 1:21
John 1:25

Romans 11:2

James 5:17

See also Revelation 11:1-12

Appendix 3
Resources

For books and other material in English on Carmelite spirituality in general and on the Elijah tradition in particular, two excellent resources are ICS Publications, a ministry of the Washington Province of the Discalced Carmelite Friars and their Institute of Carmelite Studies, and the Carmelite Institute, a joint project of the five North American Carmelite Provinces of friars, the Carmelite nuns, other Carmelite religious communities and the Lay and Secular Carmelite communities.

ICS Publications
2131 Lincoln Road NE
Washington, DC 20002-1199
Web site: http://icspublications.org

Carmelite Institute
Hecker Center, Suite #10
3025 Fourth Street NE
Washington, DC 20017-1102
Web site: http://www.carmeliteinstitute.org